SECRETS OF THE STATE
... AND HOW TO GET THEM

Richard Dowling

The Liffey Press

Published by
The Liffey Press Ltd
Ashbrook House
10 Main Street, Raheny
Dublin 5, Ireland
www.theliffeypress.com

A catalogue record of this book is
available from the British Library.

ISBN 978-1-908308-02-3

Contents

Acknowledgements

I WISH TO THANK THE **Information Commissioner**, Emily O'Reilly, and her hard working staff, in particular Fintan Butler, for their time, assistance and expertise. However, any errors or omissions in this book remain my responsibility.

I would also like to thank David Givens at The Liffey Press for his foresight in seeing the need for a book like this to encourage and assist, even if it is only in a very small way, a more open and transparent society.

Finally, to those who have to deal with Freedom of Information and AIE requests, may your toil be recognised and a predisposition to openness be rewarded.

This book could not have been written without the help and forbearance of my family, particularly my wife Ruth, as well as Beth and Jack, who put up with my disappearance for many hours over many days and for the incessant tapping on the keyboard when other things needed to be done.

This book is dedicated to them from my heart.

Foreword

RICHARD DOWLING'S BOOK ON Freedom of Information (FOI) law in Ireland is very timely in view of the Government's commitment to the renewal and extension of our FOI Act. The Government has promised 'to extend Freedom of Information . . . to ensure that all statutory bodies, and all bodies significantly funded from the public purse, are covered'. I understand that preparatory work is already underway within the Department of Public Expenditure and Reform and I very much hope that new FOI legislation will be a reality in the near future.

Looking back at 13 years of FOI in operation in Ireland, I am absolutely clear that it has achieved a great deal and that, in particular, it has changed people's expectation of what they should know about how we are governed. Whether it be the expenses of politicians and public officials, or the advice given on the economy to senior Ministers, there is now an expectation that this type of information must be released. In his book Richard encourages people to use FOI (as well as the arrangements for accessing environmental information) in a sensible and informed way. He also has some quite critical things to say about our existing legislation and about the manner in which it is applied by some public bodies. While I do not necessarily share all of his views, I recognise the sense of frustration that lies behind many of his critical comments.

We have come a considerable distance in terms of openness and accountability in government but there is still some distance to go. A renewed and extended FOI Act will play a major part in achieving this.

Richard Dowling is well qualified to produce this book and to advise both the public generally, as well as his own media colleagues, on how best to use the FOI Act. I recall being struck some years ago by one of Richard's RTÉ News pieces, based on information received under FOI, where he gave very interesting information on the Garda assessment of the possibility of foreign terrorist groups being based in Ireland. I was surprised that our FOI Act was being interpreted so liberally – not least because An Garda Síochána is not yet covered by the FOI Act! To my surprise, it transpired that Richard had got his information by way of a FOI request to the US State Department using the FOI Act of the United States. Clearly, he knows how to use FOI . . .

Emily O'Reilly
Information Commissioner
August 2011

1

The History of
Freedom of Information

I N THE LIST OF GREAT CIVIL RIGHTS campaigners the name Anders
Chydenius probably will not feature too highly. In fact, he
probably will not feature at all.

But this pastor, doctor, politician and radical from what is now
Finland played a crucial role in creating one of the most important
pieces of legislation. It has shone a light into the darkest recesses of
governments, exposed corruption and wrong doing but perhaps even
more importantly, has allowed citizens in many countries to see and
understand what their government is doing and why. Anders Chydenius is, quite simply, the father of Freedom of Information.

Here in Ireland, for example, we have Chydenius to thank for
giving us the ability to find out many things that the State, and
some of those involved in running it, would prefer we did not
know. But while FOI requests by journalists understandably make
the headlines, most users of the Act have been ordinary citizens
seeking records and information about themselves. For example,
hundreds of former residents of religious institutions were able to
find out what records existed of them while every day people make
requests seeking information such as interview records or
assessments.

The first Freedom of Information law was declared in Sweden. It now exists in various forms in approximately 85 countries around the world and is slowly working its way into transnational bodies like the European Union, International Monetary Fund and World Bank.

It is impossible to overstate the importance of this legislation. Every day it gives citizens information about their government, it exposes problems, wrong doing or waste in some organisation somewhere in the world. It has, on many occasions, had a huge political impact, for example the row over the former Ceann Comhairle, John O'Donoghue, and his spending while in office, or the controversy surrounding the expenses of elected repre- sentatives both in Ireland and in the Houses of Parliament in London.

Over the years more and more State information is published on a regular basis but not, by any means, all of it. Freedom of Information is legislation that encourages citizens to actively use it to find out details for themselves. It is one of very few laws that gives power to the people. It is also a law that requires civil and public servants to be just that – servants to the public and not the State apparatus which, unfortunately, is often the case in many instances.

It is also a transnational law in that it goes beyond the boundaries of individual states. For example, an Irish citizen can make an application under FOI legislation in the UK, the US or most other countries which have the law in their statutes. Likewise, people from outside of Ireland can make applications under FOI to public bodies here as well.

And it is also an international law, reflected in Article 19 of the Universal Declaration of Human Rights, which states that 'everyone has the right to freedom of opinion and expression; this right in- cludes freedom to hold opinions without interference and to seek, receive and impart information and ideas through any media and regardless of frontiers'.

And all this can be traced back to a cold winter's day in Sweden. The world's first Freedom of Information Act came into being on December 2, 1766 when Adolphus Frederick, the King of Sweden – a kingdom which then comprised much of modern Finland – passed 'His Majesty's Gracious Ordinance relating to Freedom of Writing and of the Press'. It would take nearly 200 years before it reached the shores of America, and 232 years before it became law in Ireland.

Somewhat bizarrely, it all started with a man of the cloth and a row over sailing rights in Sweden. The people from the province of Ostrobothnia wanted the right to send their goods to where ever they wanted and not just to the two ports they had to by law, Stockholm and Turku. Chydenius was a Lutheran pastor in the province at the time. Although his first writings concerned issues such as the overgrowing of meadows by moss and improvements in the design of horse carriages, he soon moved on to social issues and became a campaigner for openness in trade, commerce and politics.

He was already something of a local activist, clearing local marshes, experimenting with new breeds of animals and new crops. He also practiced medicine, including conducting cataract operations and fighting smallpox.

In 1765 he was elected to the Swedish Diet (Parliament) where he became the prime architect for the world's first Freedom of Information Act, which in Swedish was known as *Offentlighets-principen* – 'the principle of publicity'.

The original Act as published is, in many regards, far more liberal than its modern Irish counterpart created hundreds of years later. The 1766 Act stated that it covered all records of courts, government departments, administrators and public bodies and that records should be released to anybody who requests them. Any official who failed to comply or obstructs such a request was to lose their job.

The Act also stated that all applications, projects and proposals, reports, appeals with decisions and responses to them from societies, public bodies as well as private individuals should be available for release to the public.

The original Irish FOI Act, while a good start, went nowhere near such openness. There are many restrictions, both in the Act and in its interpretation, as well as omissions which limit what is released. For example, the gardaí, vocational education committees, National Treasury Management Agency, National Asset Management Agency, and the entire asylum process are all exempt from FOI. No convincing reason has ever been given for this, but the more parts of the State that are outside of FOI, then the easier it is for them to operate without overt public scrutiny. Who benefits?

The road to implementation in Ireland first really began in the early 1980s. There was a growing mood for openness in Irish society at the time and at a conference for higher civil servants in 1983, support was pledged to a public information act as it would dispel the mystery and secrecy which surrounded the work of the civil service.

Two years later, the Oireachtas Joint Committee on Legislation agreed to seek submissions on whether Ireland should have a Freedom of Information law. Later that year, then Senator Brendan Ryan put forward a private members bill on such a law. Needless to say, it got nowhere.

Then came the Beef Tribunal. Set up in 1991, it looked into irregularities in Ireland's beef export trade and the involvement of politicians. The Tribunal highlighted the need for more openness and transparency in Ireland's civil service. The Tribunal Chairman,

Mr. Justice Liam Hamilton, said if questions were answered in the Dáil they way they were answered at the Tribunal, there would have been no need to set it up in the first place.

In 1992, the incoming coalition Government of Fianna Fáil and the Labour Party pledged to 'consider' introducing an FOI law. A year later a campaign called 'Let in the Light' was founded with the aim of highlighting the pervasive secrecy and hidden censorship in the country at the time.

When the 'Rainbow' Coalition of Fine Gael, Labour and Democratic Left took office in 1994 there was a definite commitment to Freedom of Information on the basis that the relationship between the government and citizens had been damaged by a lack of openness. Two years later, Minister of State in the Office of the Tanaiste, Eithne Fitzgerald TD, introduced the country's first Freedom of Information Act in December. It was finally enacted in April 1997 and became law on April 21, 1998.

Interestingly, Fianna Fáil, which at the time was in Opposition, argued that this Act was not as radical as it should be and was, in fact, more restrictive than the one they'd tried to introduce as a Private Members Bill in 1995.

Speaking in the Dáil on March 11, 1997, Willie O'Dea TD said the new bill was

> '. . . a grave disappointment. It is a minimalist, carefully hedged in Bill which, if interpreted in a certain way, will make very little practical difference to the administration of this country. The long list of exemptions and cop-out clauses are so vague and imprecise that they can be interpreted as the bureaucracy wishes.'

He added that a far more radical approach was needed or 'secrecy and obfuscation will continue to flourish'.

Needless to say, when the Fianna Fáil/Progressive Democrat coalition took power they did not open up the Act. In fact, when

the coalition Government gutted large parts of the Act in 2003, all
the Party members trooped through the Lobby to support the
weakening of a Bill they had already criticised for its weakness.

Initially, the FF/PD Coalition had embraced the Act. Speaking
on April 21, 1998, the then Taoiseach, Bertie Ahern said Government institutions 'must command the full confidence and support
of the people they serve. Otherwise democracy loses out.'

However, a few years later there was an effective about-turn on
the issue when in 2003 the Freedom of Information (Amendment)
Act was passed. Amendment is a polite word for what was actually
done to the Act – its effectiveness was dramatically reduced and
blatant obstacles put in the way of those who sought to exercise
their right to access information.

A High Level Review Group comprising senior civil servants
conducted an examination – in secret – of how the Act was
functioning. This was undertaken in advance of the deadline which
would have resulted in Cabinet papers from five years earlier
becoming available. The Government in power was made up of
people who were in Cabinet five years earlier, so the outcome was
predictable. The Group didn't seek the views of anyone else but
instead 'drew upon their own experiences and experiences of others
of which they were aware, including that of their respective
Ministers'.

Unsurprisingly, they recommended substantial changes to the
Act – particularly in what information could be accessed – and they
doubled the five year limit on Cabinet papers to ten years. Perhaps
the most crucial part of the new amended Act was the introduction
of fees. It now costs €15.00 to make a non-personal application
(although several requests to one body can be included in that
application), €75.00 for an internal appeal and then €150.00 for an
appeal to the Information Commissioner. According to the
Commissioner, the introduction of these fees has had a dramatic

impact on FOI with a significant drop-off in the number of requests being made – most likely exactly what was hoped for when the changes were made.

Introducing the Amended 2003 Bill to the Dáil on March 25 of that year, the then Minister for Finance, Charlie McCreevy, defended the move claiming that the Government was not trying to repeal or blunt the original legislation but added:

> 'Freedom of Information is important. But, at the same time, it cannot be allowed to interfere with how the Government does its business efficiently in the interests of the whole community.'

This translates as 'giving the public information about what we do is not important – what is important is keeping the work of Government at all levels away from prying eyes as much as possible'. It must be a source of amazement then to all that the governments of many other countries function – and function very well – under the public gaze of much more liberal Freedom of Information legislation.

It is also worth noting that a proposal to introduce fees in the UK for FOI applications was dropped by the former Labour Government because, according to Gordon Brown, they would have placed 'unacceptable barriers' between the public and public information. And, unlike their Irish counterparts, the British government decided that Cabinet papers, and the police, should be subject to FOI.

Given the fact that our civil service and governmental system are inherited from Britain, it makes the Irish exclusions from FOI even more telling. What message does our restrictive Act send out to its citizens about the real intentions of those who run the country? What message does it sent out about letting the light shine on the inner workings of the State? There can be only one answer.

Unsurprisingly, there was much criticism of the changes introduced in the 2003 Amendment from Opposition politicians, citizens, the media and even the OECD, which in its review of the public service entitled 'Ireland: Towards an Integrated Public Service', said that the government should reduce barriers to public information by making all requests under FOI free. 'Greater transparency should be an ongoing objective even if it can sometimes be uncomfortable and/or costly,' the report states. That report, and opposition to the changes, made no difference. The amended Act went through and is still in place.

The introduction of fees, it was claimed, was necessary to deter frivolous or 'trawling' requests, both of which would take up too much civil service time and divert staff from their real work. The then Minister for Finance, Charlie McCreevy, said the fees were introduced to deter such abuse of the Act and to 'reflect some degree the work involved in processing a request'. This was spin put out to achieve a simple aim – political cover for a reduction in the scope of this citizen's law.

If the Government had such issues with frivolous or 'trawling' requests they could look to Section 10 of the FOI Act, which allows requests to be refused on administrative grounds, including that it would cost a substantial amount of money to answer a request or that it would result in unreasonable interference with the running of a public body. Presumably, Section 10 could easily be used to prevent organisations falling asunder as a result of FOI requests. The other alternative would have been to publish a lot more information, make as many records available as possible so people would not have to submit FOI requests in the first place. Neither were viable options. It was just a lot easier and far more effective to limit the scope of the Act.

In 2008 the Department of Finance estimated the cost of processing an FOI request was around €485.00. Based on that figure, the total cost of running FOI legislation from its inception up to 2009 would amount to €66.6 million according to Dr. Nat O'Connor from TASC in a paper called, 'An economic argument for stronger Freedom of Information Laws in Ireland'. In 2009 alone, the State spent €56 billion running the country, of which €6.9 million went on Freedom of Information. 'That does not seem to be an exorbitant price to pay for stronger democratic oversight of public spending,' Dr. O'Connor notes.

The fees imposed for FOI requests brought in €115,000 for 2009, while it cost €6.9 million to operate the legislation and, according to Dr. O'Connor, the cost of collecting and processing the fees is more than they actually bring in.

While fees like this are an Irish phenomenon, one common thread that runs through Freedom of Information legislation from its very inception is the politician's promise that is made every time it becomes law in any country – that it will transform the work of the State and its officials and provide a deeper understanding to the people of how they are governed. From King Adolphus Frederick of Sweden through to President Lyndon B. Johnson (who despised the idea of FOI), Bertie Ahern and Tony Blair, they have all said that FOI would lead to greater understanding by citizens of the work of the State, as well as hold civil servants and politicians to account by scrutinising what they do with public money.

While the words are similar, the impact differs widely, mainly due to the strength of the legislation and the willingness of the participants around the world to cooperate with it. The crucial question is, has the Act improved how we are governed here in Ireland? How decisions are made regarding public money? And how well the public understand what has happened and why? An optimist will say it has improved things significantly. A realist might say it probably has brought about some changes but there is much, much more to do.

The simple truth is that the civil service has worked on behalf of the State and its citizens since its foundation without the prying eyes of journalists and the public. We have only had FOI legislation for the last few years so it is probably unrealistic to expect a dramatic transformation in the practice and, more importantly, in the mindset of civil servants.

There are many working for the State who truly believe that the public has a right to access as much information as possible. In my view, however, they are not the majority. The view still holds sway that the less the public knows the easier it is for civil servants to do their job. In that regard, they are probably right. If we knew the full picture of what was going on, if there was close public scrutiny, then it could make their jobs and the jobs of their political masters more difficult. But when we are talking about public money is that necessarily a bad thing?

Only time and regular use of the Act, even if it is reduced in scope and power, will tell if change has come to the previously secretive operations of the State at national and local level. There are, however, grounds for hope. The Fine Gael/Labour coalition has pledged to restore the Act to its previous strength by removing the restrictions put in place, and has also promised to extend its scope to many public bodies which are currently outside its remit, especially in the area of finance.

If these changes are carried out, it will mark a fundamental shift in the influence of citizens in public administration. It will allow each and every one to participate, to discover and to understand what is going on in this State. If the Act is extended to financial bodies such as the Central Bank and the National Treasury Management Agency, it will allow ordinary people and journalists to see inside the mandarins' palace – a place where currently only the select few know what is going on with the billions of euro that taxpayers are obliged to provide.

One of the reasons for our economic crisis is that those in charge of monitoring the banks either did not know or did not ask the right questions. If they were subject to FOI, would they have taken such a hands-off approach? It is highly likely the media, for example, would have submitted requests to find out what was going on and raised concerns, but they were not able to do so because the bodies involved are outside the remit of the Act. Transparency may have made a difference, but we will never know.

As Emily O'Reilly, the Information Commissioner, said in a speech to a joint meeting of the Archives and Records Association Ireland and the Information and Records Management Society of Ireland, 'in a democratic society it is proper that those who wield power – whether political, administrative or economic – should be open to the scrutiny of an informed public'. The question, she said, is 'would the scale of the (economic) devastation have been less or even been avoided completely, had we a stronger regime of transparency in place?'

In fairness, there should also be criticism leveled at the media in terms of how the Act has been used. There was, for example, much use of the Act to find out trivial information, such as the cost of former Taoiseach Bertie Ahern's make-up bill.

But then there were also other occasions when the Act was used to powerful effect, such as the investigations into spending at FÁS. We also regularly see stories emerging as a result of FOI from the Health Service Executive about problems or concerns about our hospitals. In fact, as a result of FOI inspection reports on nursing homes, crèches and politicians' expenses are now regularly being published.

The Irish Act, although not as open as its Swedish counterpart, is still quite useful. With skillful use it can allow citizens or businesses to see what decisions have been made and – more importantly – why. It can also show the reasoning used by public bodies to reach a decision so people or companies can see some of the 'thought processes' that go on internally.

Given the importance of national and local government, as well as the influence of the European Union, there is no doubt that examining what people do on behalf of citizens – why they do it and how much they spend doing it – is of huge importance. And it is not just up to journalists to find out such information. If you want to know more about something, there's nothing to stop you trying to get access to the primary source – the information itself - without it being 'filtered' by the media.

This is your money that is being spent. It is your right to know what is being done with it. We should be confident that tax revenue is well spent on our behalf. Are you reassured this is the case? If not, ask yourself why not, and what can you do about it. Why bother, is the frequent answer, I will not be able to change anything.

Well, in fact you can. With determination and, in many cases, a dogged will to pursue an issue, you can make a difference. You can do it to learn more, to understand for yourself what is happening. You don't have to be a journalist to publish your efforts. There are many websites that would love to report new information about a particular topic, especially if it is newsworthy.

In a speech to mark the tenth anniversary of the Act, the Information Commissioner said that the vast majority of people and much of the media will continue to be reliant on the 'official' information services. She went on:

> 'But it is vital, in my view, that FOI continues to be available for those in the media, for lobby groups, for community groups and for those ordinary people who, for whatever reason, want to decide for themselves on the information they should have and want to receive that information in an unmediated fashion.'

There is, it must be said, much scope for journalists to use the Act to produce more stories or obtain more detail on issues. It does take time and determination, particularly if the body refuses to release the information, and it is not always guaranteed to produce results. However, it should be on every journalist's agenda to learn about, and to use, legislation that allows access to State records – not to rely on the official line, but to delve deeper and find out what is really been going on.

Those involved in running campaigns or lobbying on specific issues can also use the legislation to find out more from local, national or international bodies. Having too much information never damages a campaign . . . having too little, on the other hand, certainly will. If, for example, you access unpublished reports or simple documents which come to the same conclusions as your campaign, your chances of convincing others that you are correct is much stronger. Similarly, if you can access records to show that, for example, an alternative route for a road was cheaper or less obtrusive to build, then you have a convincing argument that could lead to changes being made.

There is also huge commercial potential possible by accessing such information. While FOI has clauses to protect commercial interests, it is still quite possible to get reports that could inform you of how a particular body has looked at an issue, or what experts have said to them on this topic. All of this could be of huge benefit when it comes to planning a future strategy.

The Act also allows access to reports prepared for a public body by outside contractors, which can be very useful, particularly if a final decision has not yet been made. For example, a company could see what internal reports are suggesting and adapt all or part of their business as necessary.

Academics too should use FOI more for their own research and to understand why a particular approach has been adopted by a public body. Many academics often appear in the media or online commenting about Government decisions or likely decisions. How much better it would be if, in addition to bringing their expertise to bear on a particular decision, they could also use FOI to learn more about what is going on within a department or organisation. This inevitably would take time because FOI in Ireland is particularly slow in comparison to other countries, but it would allow deeper analysis of State activity.

In an era when the marketplace is global and the influences on domestic life can come from other continents, using FOI internationally can be an invaluable tool to access information and understand what is happening or what is likely to occur. So don't be afraid to practice FOI outside of these shores. The extent of FOI legislation varies from country to country so it is also worth examining closely the FOI regimes in other States as possible sources of information relating to Ireland. In fact, it is often the case that what may be deemed too sensitive for release here, or even be outside the remit of the Act here, is available in other countries.

For example, I obtained a list of suspected extremist Islamic terror groups which the gardaí believed were operating in Ireland under Freedom of Information. The Garda Siochána remains outside FOI here and that information would never have been released in a million years from the Department of Justice. The information in this case came from an FOI request I made to the US State Department. America has a far more liberal FOI regime and together with the fact that Ireland is relatively unimportant on the world stage this meant the information could be released without causing consternation.

Other countries like Sweden and Finland have an even more open approach. In these countries it is possible to see letters written to and by the Prime Minister to other heads of state. It is possible to see letters and e-mails sent to and from the civil service within hours of being created. Here in Ireland such open disclosure is unlikely, so it might be worthwhile to put in FOI requests to other countries to see what our Government is saying to them.

It is also likely that legislation allowing public access will be introduced at some stage to transnational bodies like the World Bank and the International Monetary Fund, for example. There are tentative steps in this direction, but they are a long way from being open and transparent to the ordinary citizen.

While the Freedom of Information Act is the bedrock for openness, there are other pieces of legislation which the private citizen, journalist or business can use to access records. There is an EU directive, Accessing Information on the Environment (AIE), which, potentially, has much wider scope both in terms of information that can be accessed and the bodies from which that information can be garnered. This is in place in most EU countries and, like FOI, requests can be made to other countries as well as to our own State. The Information Commissioner, Emily O'Reilly, has spoken on several occasions about the scope and effectiveness of the directive. 'It does,' she said, 'offer great potential . . . if only it was used more often.' Speaking to journalism students in Limerick, the Information Commissioner said:

> 'The regulations were enacted a number of years ago, yet so far there is precious little usage of the Access right either by the public or by the media. This is partly because of unfamiliarity with the regulations, and also a lack of awareness of how they differ in scope from the provisions of the FOI act.'

> 'Each exemption, for example, is subject to a public interest test, and the range of bodies covered is much greater than in FOI. Given the supposed great public interest in the environment, I think the media might do well to ex-

amine this access route to information and begin to use
it.'

And then there is EU Directive 1049/2001, which supposedly
allows access to internal EU documents. There is much deserved
criticism of the lack of openness and transparency within EU
institutions, which include a vast network of organisations with a
myriad of offshoots. Getting information using this route is very
much a hit and miss affair . . . generally a miss. The EU and its
institutions seem to have an exceptionally strong aversion to
releasing information in an uncontrolled way.

For example, a Maltese journalist and I tried to get details of
MEPs' expense claims but were refused under the guise that
releasing figures (I only wanted total amounts) could identify
members of their staff – even though I specifically said such names
were not part of my request. MEPs' expenses are soon to be made
freely available, but only due to the Parliament releasing the
information.

But regardless of the obstacles, these are citizen's laws – they
are your tools to use. There are many phrases bandied about on
how this is the Age of Information and that Information is King,
but despite their hackneyed overuse there is a good deal of truth in
them. Imperfect as they all are, it is up to each and every one of us
to use the laws to the utmost.

It is only by regularly exercising this fundamental human right
that we can change the mindset of those who control the
information, and enshrine the view that it is our right to know how
and what is done in our name and with our money.

It is a true citizen's law. It is there for you to use . . . so use it.

2

The Freedom of Information Act

SECRECY HAS ALWAYS BEEN of paramount importance for the State. Up until the passing of the Freedom of Information Act in 1997, the main law governing the release of information about the State was the Official Secrets Act. That was aimed at preventing information being given out to the public about what the State was doing – quite the opposite of FOI. It meant that politicians and civil servants were the only people who told the public what was going on, usually through the media.

This obviously was good for the politicians and senior civil servants because it meant they could release information that favoured them and hide information that did not. This was, however, inherently bad for the public because they did not know what was going on behind the scenes and because the media were only fed titbits of information if and when it suited the powers that be.

But according to some experts this has not changed all that much despite FOI. 'Irish ministers and government departments are surrounded by excessive secrecy,' according to Dr. Nat O'Connor who wrote a report entitled 'The role of access to information in Ireland's democracy'. The report for TASC, an independent Irish think tank 'dedicated to combating Ireland's high level of economic inequality', was published in 2010. Dr. O'Connor noted that there is still a pervasive culture of secrecy in the Irish civil service which poses serious problems. As he points out:

> 'Open Government may present a challenge to our politicians and public servants but it is not a threat. It is not an optional extra. Secret government, hidden information and blanket confidentiality are all inextricably linked to bad decisions and bad government.'

For example, even in countries with similar traditional civil service establishments like the UK and Australia, cabinet papers are instantly subject to FOI. Initially in Ireland they could only be accessed after five years, but then the former Government introduced changes to the Act to ensure cabinet papers could only be released after ten years.

Changing the culture of secrecy will take time, as will wider acceptance of the idea of the public's right to the information they want – rather than what the government or apparatus of the State thinks they should have. Only bit by bit, with more and more people using FOI will this mindset change. As noted earlier, it is everyone's right, and I would argue everyone's duty, to demand more information about what is done in their name and with their money.

In July, 2011 the United Nations Human Rights Committee declared that as part of the human right to access information, governments should:

> '. . . proactively put in the public domain Government information of public interest. State parties should make every effort to ensure easy, prompt, effective and practical access to such information.'

In their General Comment No. 34, the UNHRC goes on to state that 'fees for requests for information should not be such as to constitute an unreasonable impediment to access'.

However, despite all this and the many positive aspects to FOI, archivists and historians have begun to highlight a serious problem with how it is implemented in reality by civil servants. It's called 'Open Access – Empty Archives'. The problem is that civil servants and politicians could become reluctant to commit discussions, advice or opinions to any form of permanent record because it could be subject to FOI.

The former head of the Swedish National Audit Office, Inga-Britt Ahlenius, said Freedom of Information has led to fewer opportunities for scrutiny in Sweden. She has argued that most of what is of greatest interest is simply not written down. She asked a number of senior Swedish business people whether they had written to their Government on a matter that was really important to them. The answer, she said, was no because important issues are discussed orally. This obviously means there are no written records, which is a problem both for people seeking information under FOI as well as archivists and historians doing research with a longer timeframe.

There is anecdotal evidence that this is happening in Ireland too, but probably not to such an extent yet and hopefully it won't become endemic. It is, in my view, unacceptable that people employed by the State to carry out work on behalf of its citizens should adopt such an approach. They are not involved in running a secret society; they are involved in running an open society. What is there to fear from committing to a record their reasons, their views and their decisions? If they are honest (and there is no reason to believe they are not), then there can be nothing to fear from public scrutiny. If, for example, they are proven wrong on a certain matter, then as long as there is a record to show how and why a decision was made then there can be no allegations levelled against them. If there are no such records, surely they leave themselves open to claims of wrongdoing or ineptitude.

While this problem has been well vented in Sweden, which has had a Freedom of Information Act for centuries, here in Ireland we've only had an FOI Act for a couple of years. Although it was originally called the Freedom of Information Act 1997, it actually came into force on April 21, 1998 for Government Departments and many Governmental bodies. This means that only information created from this date onwards is available under Freedom of Information. There is an exception to this rule, though. If, to get a full picture of an event or decision, it is necessary to release records created before that date, then they can be under the Act. With the passage of time, however, it is less and less likely that this will become an issue.

While it is called a Freedom of Information Act, it is, in reality, a Freedom of Records Act. A person may have information that is not written down, such as details passed to them in a conversation, but that is not subject to FOI. The Act is clear where it says it provides a right of access to records and then defines what a record actually is: a memorandum, book, plan, map, drawing, diagram, pictorial or graphic work or other document, any photograph, film or record whether it is stored manually, mechanically or electronically. This obviously includes reports, documents and e-mails, but would also include phone texts and other material held on mobile phones, for example.

While most main organs of the State came under FOI from April 1998, the health boards as they were at the time and local authorities such as town and county councils came under Freedom of Information on October 21, 1998, meaning that only records created by them from that date onwards are subject to FOI.

The extremely long opening sentence of the Act outlines its purpose in what is tortured legalistic phraseology. Its aim is to 'enable members of the public to access, to the greatest extent possible, consistent with the public interest and right to privacy, information in the possession of public bodies'. This is the key to FOI – the power is given to the citizen to access information held by the State. It also allows people to access personal information held by bodies through FOI and, if there's a mistake, they can have it corrected.

The basic broad principle of the Act, therefore, is that decisions of public bodies should be more open to public scrutiny with the aim proving greater appreciation of the issues involved in policy decisions leading to stronger public ownership and acceptance of decisions made. People affected by decisions of public bodies have a right to know the criteria used in making the decision and people have a right to know what information is held by the Government or State about them and correct errors if there are any.

The Act is broken down into five separate parts:

○ Part 1: Preliminary and General, which sets out the purpose of the Act, regulations involved and definitions of words in the Act such as what is a 'record' and 'exempt records', for example

○ Part 2: Access to Records, which sets out the details of how people can apply for information and what should happen next, internal appeals and so on

○ Part 3: Exempt Records, which lists the grounds on which a Department or body can refuse to release information

○ Part 4: The role of the Information Commission and the powers that go with the office

○ Part 5: Miscellaneous, which details, for example, measures to follow for appeals to the High Court, granting immunity from prosecution for releasing information under FOI and, most importantly, setting out specific areas which are exempt from the Act such as courts, tribunals and the office of the President.

It is primarily Parts 2 and 3, as well as some of Part 5, that those interested in submitting requests need to understand in any great detail.

Government departments and State organisation produce thousands of pages of material every working day. The vast bulk of these are unlikely to be of general interest. But even so, that still leaves a lot of records that could be of public or personal interest.

You can request (although you may not necessarily get) any record held by the Government, local authority or many of the other State organisations that are subject to the Act. For example, you could ask to get the minutes of meetings, reports or copies of letters and e-mails between certain offices or specific people. If a report has been published, or even if it has not, you can ask for all the documents that relate to it such as correspondence received and any internal memos.

A particular area to note is that organisations often employ outside contractors to do some work for them. If the organisation itself is subject to FOI, then what these contractors do on its behalf is subject to the Act as well. And it's not just limited to a final report that they may have drawn up, but all draft reports and associated documents which helped form those reports are subject to the Act.

Anyone around the world can submit an FOI request in Ireland. It can be sent directly to the relevant public authority or it can also be sent to an Irish embassy overseas as it represents Ireland in that particular country. You do not have to give a reason and you won't be asked for one. It is a core principle of FOI that everyone is equal and that requests should be considered on their own merits. What you do with the information you receive is also not a matter for question when you submit your FOI request.

When an FOI officer has to decide whether to release information or not, they are not supposed to consider any such issue – the decisions are supposed to be 'applicant blind' in that it does not matter if you are journalist, a politician or a member of the public, the considerations that have to be made about releasing the records are to be the same in all circumstances. However, it is quite likely that this is not the case in reality, as the identity of those making the requests is an issue in some cases.

The Department of the Environment, Community and Local Government publishes some details of FOI requests, describing the requestor in general terms such as 'business' or 'journalist'. The Department of Communications, Energy and Natural Resources goes much further. It publishes the name and address of the requestor (if the person makes the request in a professional capacity – especially journalists), but then they also publish the information they release under FOI. It is all available on their website for everyone to see. This, the Attorney General has assured them, is legal. Critics have argued that this was another crude attempt, particularly by the Department of Communications, to hamper journalists because the information they get can be the basis of a story. However, since it is also released to everyone else it is possible that others could publish the information before the journalist who actually submitted the request, thereby reducing the inclination to make requests in the first place. However, most Government departments and agencies that are subject to FOI do not publish details of the requestor or the released documents on their websites.

The other area where the issue of the identity of the requestor is a factor relates to the area of personal information. It is obvious and only fair that if a person is seeking information held about themselves it should be easier to obtain than if a complete stranger was seeking the same records.

FOI Exemptions

There are two types of exemptions to FOI – 'mandatory' and 'discretionary'. Mandatory exemptions mean the official deciding on a request does not have a choice in the matter. They may feel the information requested should be released, but if it falls into a specific category (such as Government records) the request must be refused.

The other type of exemption is 'discretionary', which means the deciding officer has to decide whether to release the information or not. That decision will depend on a variety of conditions such as what information is being sought, timing and the public interest. Refusals on almost all grounds can be appealed internally and then to the Information Commissioner if necessary.

There are also two types of bodies subject to FOI – organisations which are entirely within the remit of the Act, such as local authorities and Government Departments, and ones (usually related to the legal world) which are only partially subject to FOI. These include the Courts Service, tribunals and legal offices of the State, for example.

Records created during the day-to-day work of the courts and tribunals are automatically excluded from FOI as they could lead to interference with the course of justice. Section 40 of the Commission of Investigations 2004 Act specifically states that the FOI Act does not apply to an investigation or tribunal set up under its remit, except where the records being sought were created before the order was signed establishing the Commission or if the request relates to the general administration, including expenses, of the Commission.

However, there's a sting in the tail of this Act as it allows for the exemption to continue to exist long after the tribunal or commission has finished its work. It states that all records created and received are exempt if they're held by the Commission, by a Minister or by anyone who holds the records after a tribunal of inquiry has been dissolved. So even twenty years after a tribunal has ceased to exist, records created by it will still be exempt under this Act.

But records which, for example, related to the running of the tribunals or courts in general are subject to FOI. This allows access to information like concerns over staffing or how much legal counsel gets paid, for example. It's a similar story too for the office of the Director of Public Prosecutions, the Attorney General, the Comptroller and Auditor General and the office of the Ombudsman. You will not be able to get to see records they have about their actual work, but you can access information about the running of these offices.

Certain individuals who work for the State have total exemption from FOI. These include TDs and Senators – they can make requests under the Act but their own personal and professional papers are totally exempt. The office of the President and all records relating to it, from whatever organisation, are also totally outside the remit of the Freedom of Information Act.

Exclusions, mandatory and discretionary, exist not only in the Irish Act but in most acts worldwide. They are there to allow the organisation to refuse to release information if they feel it necessary for a variety of reasons such as security, to protect personal information or if the release would harm international relations, to mention but a few.

Most of the exemptions, especially the ones created or strengthened in the 2003 Amendment, are aimed at protecting the Government and the core decision making parts of the State. For example, in the Amendment there was a huge expansion of what a 'government' actually means. For most people the Government is the Cabinet, but as a result of the changes introduced in 2003 the definition of the word under the Act was extended to a vast array of committees and sub-committees which need not even have a Cabinet member serving on them.

This dramatically changed Freedom of Information in Ireland in a way which restricted access to suit the politicians and senior civil servants. The changes followed a 'review' which was carried out by the civil service without public involvement and was clearly designed to protect them and their political masters.

Part 3 of the Act, which sets out exempt records, was the focus of most attention by this review process. For example, the original Act said Cabinet papers could be available after five years, but this was doubled to ten years. Possible discretion by decision makers in other areas was removed with the words 'may refuse' being changed to the instruction 'shall refuse'.

Overall, the changes in the 2003 Amendment vastly increased the scope of records which 'shall be refused', and effectively demonstrated the complete disregard to the ideals of transparency and openness in the running of this country.

And then there has been the huge increase in quangos (quasi-autonomous non-governmental organisations) to which the Government has delegated much of the work formally done by departments. Of course, while the departments are subject to FOI many of the quangos are not, which means there is precious little transparency about their work.

There are over 500 organisations which are subject to FOI, including all Government departments as well as all local authorities, the HSE, third level educational institutes and universities. However, many of the 500 plus organisations which are subject to the Act are not likely to be hugely important to the running of the State and can best be described as having only a sectoral interest. These could include bodies such as the Commissioner of Valuation and Boundary Surveyor for Ireland, the Local Government Computer Services Board and the National Milk Agency.

There are, however, many notable exclusions from the Act as a result of what has been a deliberate policy to keep them outside the remit of independent public scrutiny. These include bodies such as the An Garda Siochána, the Vocational Education Committees, the Refugee Applications Commissioner and the Office of the Refugee Tribunal, to mention but a few. There has never been a convincing reason given for these remaining outside the Act, and although the Information Commissioner, Emily O'Reilly, has raised this on many occasions, previous governments have shown little interest in extending the Act to cover them.

For example, the forerunner to the Health and Safety Authority was the National Authority for Occupational Safety and Health. That was fully subject to FOI, but when it was replaced by the HSA the FOI was limited to just administration – putting it on a par with the likes of a tribunal or other legal body. This curtailment was done by hiding the exclusion deep within the text of the legislation which set up the HSA so no one noticed!

There was an even more disturbing case involving the Medical Bureau of Road Safety. It was, at one stage, completely under the remit of FOI, but following a decision by the Information Commissioner relating to drink driving and accessing records, legislation was brought in which ensured that only administrative functions of the body were subject to FOI. And all of this was done without even informing the Commissioner.

Another example is the Road Safety Authority (RSA). Its forerunner was the National Safety Council, which was subject to FOI, but when the RSA was set up in 2006 it was outside the remit of the Act. The Authority claims, however, that in its approach to openness and transparency they have acted as if they were subject to FOI. While this attitude is admirable, a body *acting* like it is subject to FOI and a body which actually *is* subject to FOI are clearly completely different things. One is legally bound to treat requests for information as set out in the Act; the other can do so if it chooses.

If the Road Safety Authority was subject to FOI it would, by law, have to follow certain procedures and it would not be subject to demands from contractors. For example, when Pricewaterhouse Coopers did a report for the RSA they made demands of the Authority in advance of it possibly being made public. They insisted that if the record should be released there would have to be discussions with them in advance, and the Authority would have to have 'regard' for their views as well as include a disclaimer from PWC.

Under FOI, a public body has the power to make decisions for itself and any reports it has paid for, although it is free, of course, to discuss the release with the report's authors.

In its 2009 annual report, the Road Safety Authority said work was underway to bring it under the Act. It still has not happened.

But what is the reason for setting up new public authorities and then deliberately keeping them outside the remit of FOI? It seems it is just the way the State prefers it. The thinking seems to be that the more organisations outside the reach of FOI and public scrutiny the better.

Personal or commercially sensitive information also has fairly rigorous protection under the Act. It is understandable that the State should seek to protect such information from general release, and there are several sections within the Act which give the decision makers the power to do so. That does not mean, however, that such records cannot be released. They can and sometimes are, especially commercial information. Timing is the key issue here. If, for example, you ask for records relating to specific contracts while a competition is under way you certainly won't get them, but you might at some later point.

Many State bodies also have commercial information that is either created by themselves or passed on to them by, for example, commercial semi-state bodies. It can be considerably more difficult to get information like this from the organisation – but not impossible.

But confidentiality does not just involve commercial information – it can also include personal agreements with State bodies, and just because people believe a deal is confidential that does not actually make it so. In a significant ruling in 2005, the Information Commissioner ordered the release of details about a pay-off deal to a medical consultant in the north east despite the presence of a confidentiality clause in the agreement. The Commissioner ruled that since it was public money involved the public had a right to know what was being done with it.

The lesson is clear – do not be put off by exemptions. If you want to acquire information about something then it is simply up to you to try to get it. Remember, it is your money that is paying for the civil service and you are entitled – in most circumstances – to see what is being done on your behalf. That is the core function of the Freedom of Information Act.

FOI and the Public Interest

There is another important part of FOI and it relates to the public interest. This clause features in many sections of the Act and allows for a decision maker to look at whether the public interest is best served by releasing or not releasing information. This is very much a subjective interpretation. It is not necessarily a matter of what interests the public, but what is in the interest of the public. In other words, if it is in the general good for the records to be released, then they can and should be. This is an issue that will come up frequently in appeals against decisions to refuse or to limit information being released.

FOI in Action

You only have to look at the media to see the regular use of FOI in particular to produce news stories . . . stories which make headlines. Highlighting misuse of public money, for example, brought about major changes saving the taxpayer, while highlighting serious deficiencies in the areas of health care, such as in nursing homes, has brought about more openness and improved conditions.

There are stories on an almost daily basis where reporters access reports, letters and e-mails on a huge range of issues such as health, the environment and education which reveal previously unknown details or highlight concerns within an organisation.

But while the work of journalists makes the headlines, they represent a small fraction of the total number of requests under the Freedom of Information Act. Just over three-quarters of all requests come from individuals or representative organisations. This proves without doubt that FOI benefits most – and is most used by – the citizens of Ireland or groups representing them.

Given the events of recent years, and the dramatic downturn in relation to the state of the country's finances, it would seem that public scrutiny would be important, if not essential, to the bodies responsible for billions of euros of our money. However, this is not the case. In terms of finance there is a huge gap in the number of bodies excluded from the Act, and therefore from outside scrutiny. These include National Asset Management Agency, the National Treasury Management Agency, the Central Bank, the Financial Services Authority, the Financial Services Regulatory Authority and the State Claims Agency, to mention just a few.

Ironically, according to documents released to *The Irish Independent* under the Freedom of Information Act, it emerged that the organisation which represents banks, the Irish Banking Federation, wrote to the Department of Finance urging them to ensure NAMA was outside the remit of FOI. They got their way.

Regardless of the billions of euro guaranteed by the taxpayers, NAMA was and is covered by the enormous blanket of state secrecy and kept away from any prying eyes who might wish to see what is going on.

But that does not stop people urging change. In May of 2010, the Chairman of what was then Anglo Irish Bank, Alan Dukes, said NAMA should be subject to FOI, while the Information Commissioner, Emily O'Reilly, said not only NAMA but other financial organisations should be subject to the Act. She said that including NAMA under FOI was a 'no brainer' as it would help shore up public confidence, but its exclusion would do the opposite and undermine public trust.

So what did the State do? Did they take on board the views of those who said transparency was good, or did they take the view that the people must be kept in the dark? Given the track record of the State, it is no surprise that NAMA remains outside FOI.

These were the decisions of the previous Government and maybe things will change. But regardless, it is important to point out that the approach adopted here runs contrary to the general norm in the western world, including our nearest neighbour, the UK. There, for example, the financial arms of the Realm are generally subject to FOI, as are the police and publicly owned companies. In fact, before FOI came into force, the Metropolitan Police engaged one of the leading FOI campaigners, Maurice Frankel, to help them prepare for it.

Here, though, the attitude has been exactly the opposite. The State has sought to prevent openness and transparency by curtailing an act that was supposed to do the opposite.

Still, a reduced act is better than no act at all.

3

How to Use the Freedom of Information Act

THE ACTUAL PROCESS OF MAKING AN application under the Freedom of Information Act is relatively straightforward. Although it may seem blindingly obvious, the first thing you need to do is to decide what you are looking for, which will in turn determine to whom you submit the FOI application. For example, are you looking for a specific report and/or the records created during its compilation, the minutes of meetings or just looking to see what records exist about yourself or a specific topic?

Once you've determined what you are seeking then you need to decide who is likely to hold the records you want. Is it a Government department, local authority or some other State body? It is important to check whether that body is actually subject to the Freedom of Information Act because if not then you are just wasting your time (although depending on what you are seeking it may be possible to submit a request under the Accessing Information on the Environment regulation or Data Protection Acts). It is relatively simple to check if a body is subject to FOI. Many organisations will have on their website a link from their home page entitled 'Freedom of Information'; click on that and it will bring you to a page which details how to submit an application to them. Some organisations, however, don't have such a link. Then you will have to search their website to see if they are subject to FOI.

Other good places to get a list of organisations which are subject to FOI is the website of the Information Commissioner (www.oic. gov.ie/en/PrescribedPublicBodies) or from the Department of Public Expenditure and Reform (http://foi.gov.ie/). This Department oversees FOI and through their Freedom of Information Central Policy Unit issues notices and advice to decision makers on what to do and how to do it. This useful website not only lists all the bodies covered by the Act, but, in many cases, the person who deals with FOI applications.

Organisations which are subject to the Act are also obliged to produce what are called Section 15 and Section 16 manuals. A Section 15 manual contains a general description of the body's structure and organisation, as well as its functions, powers and duties. It also gives a general description of the types of records it holds and how these records can be accessed. This manual can be useful if you are researching a topic that one or more organisations may have a role in so that you can make an FOI request to each of them. A Section 16 manual sets out the rules, guidelines and practices an organisation uses to run itself and its staff. It is usually not of huge interest to members of the general public.

So once you have determined what you are looking for and who is likely to hold such records, you obviously then need to write to the organisation. If the request is for personal information then it is easiest to send an email to the organisation setting out what information you're seeking. If the request is for non-personal information, then it is easier to send a letter as you will have to pay a €15.00 fee to make the request. The alternative is to submit the request online and then post the fee in separately, but there is always the inherent risk of one or the other going astray somewhere along the line.

The issue of fees is important and controversial. As mentioned in Chapter One, they seem to have been introduced in a deliberate effort by the then Fianna Fáil/Progressive Democrat government to reduce the number of FOI applications being made. The Information Commissioner, Emily O'Reilly, has repeatedly criticised the fees as they can actually prevent people seeking information they should be able to get. There were proposals in the UK to introduce fees but they were dropped because the then Labour Government decided fees would act as a deterrent which would be contrary to the spirit and aims of the Act. No such qualms here though.

If the request is for non-personal information the application fee is €15.00, which then goes up steeply to €75.00 for an internal appeal within the organisation and then €150.00 for an appeal to the Information Commissioner. Such exorbitant fees clearly have the effect of dissuading people from seeking to appeal decisions. If the requestor has a medical card then the fees are €10.00 to make the application, €25.00 for an internal appeal and then €50.00 for an appeal to the Information Commissioner

If the requestor is seeking personal information about themselves, or if acting as a parent or guardian are seeking records about their family member, then there is no fee payable when making the request or at appeal stage.

In all cases, however, there may be a fee payable for search and retrieval of the records and for copying them. These can run into hundreds or even thousands of euro and a deposit will usually be sought. Once the organisation has issued a letter or an e-mail detailing how much it will cost, the clock stops on the request and nothing happens until the deposit is paid. The alternative is to appeal the imposition of expensive charges to the Information Commissioner on the grounds that they are excessive. It will then be up to the organisation to prove to the Commissioner's office that the search and retrieval charges are reasonable.

There are also fees payable if someone or some organisation wishes to appeal a decision of a public body to release information which involves them, a so called 'third party appeal'. That will cost €50.00.

Of course, along with having to pay up for the privilege of making a request or an appeal, there is no guarantee that it will produce the results you want. However, it is important to remember that obstacles are there to be overcome!

It is also important to note that you can make a number of separate and unrelated requests for information to the same organisation under one FOI application. So if, for example, you are submitting a request to a Government department you can actually ask for copies of records relating to three or four separate topics. There is, as of yet, no rule as to how many requests you can submit on payment of the one fee. Each request will be treated separately by the organisation, and you may have to pay search and retrieval fees, if imposed, on each of them.

There are three basics you need to state in your application:

o Your letter or email must state that the request for records is being made under the Freedom of Information Act

o It must contain sufficient details to allow the organisation to identify what records you are seeking

o It must contain €15.00 as the application fee or €10.00 if you have a medical card. As noted, if the request is for personal information about you or a family member then there is no fee payable.

You can specify how you wish to receive the records, that is, whether photocopied, on computer disc, by e-mail, etc. It may seem obvious if you include €15.00 cheque and ask for certain records that the request is being made under FOI, but unless it is clearly stated on the letter then it does not have to be considered by the organisation as such. Also, once a request is made under FOI then certain procedures have to be followed by the body.

The wording of your letter does not have to be overly elaborate and something along the lines of 'Under the Freedom of Information Act I would like a copy of all records relating to . . .' would suffice, or 'Under the Freedom of Information Act I would like to request a copy of the report which examined . . .' These are just sample wordings – you can use whatever form of words you like as long as you state that the request is being made under the Freedom of Information Act. And, once again, do not forget that your request can have several separate and unrelated elements to it. The one payment of €15.00 will cover them.

As regards the second element – sufficient details – you need to be reasonably specific but you do not have to know the exact details of a record you want. It is obvious that people working outside the organisation cannot be expected to know every document that has been created on a particular issue. If there is, however, a specific report or topic that you are interested in then specify it. Otherwise your request could turn up a huge number of records which may result in you being asked to narrow the scope of your request. This could take the form of limiting the dates of the request or refining the search criteria.

'Trawls', where a requestor asks for every document relating to a wide-ranging subject should generally be avoided because they can be time-consuming and costly. However, trawls on a smaller scope are perfectly acceptable. The key issue here is the scale of the request. Sometimes a request which you think could cover a huge number of documents may not actually do so as the organisation may not have that many relating to the subject. On the other hand, requests which you think would be relatively concise could, in fact, cover a lot of records.

Trawls which result in a huge number of documents being covered can easily be rejected by the organisation because the result is too voluminous. Section 10 of the Act allows a request to be rejected if retrieval and examination of such a large number of records would cause a 'substantial and unreasonable interference with or disruption of the work of the public body concerned'.

If, for example, a requestor seeks every record relating to the school building programme of the Department of Education over the last ten years, that is almost sure to be rejected on grounds that it would cause considerable disruption within the Department. However, if a requestor sought every record relating to a specific school then that is more likely to succeed because the FOI officers in the Department can precisely identify the records being sought.

Requests which a decision maker decides are 'frivolous or vexatious', or are part of a pattern of 'manifestly unreasonable requests', can also be rejected under Section 10 of the Act. There have been a number of instances where public bodies have rejected requests under this Section and those decisions have been appealed to the Information Commissioner with various outcomes.

> *A separated man sought a copy of all social welfare records held by the Eastern Health Board relating to him, his daughter and former partner with her consent. However, the health board refused the request on a variety of grounds, including that it was frivolous and vexatious because they argued that most of the information had already been released. This argument was not accepted by the Commissioner who ordered the release of further information.*

However, in another case, the Commissioner took the opposite view.

Mr. X made a request to RTÉ seeking information about Mr. Y, a cousin of his. There was an ongoing family dispute over a will between the two and it was claimed that Mr. Y's work in RTÉ was adding to Mr. X's pain and hurt. Mr. X made many requests to RTÉ which were refused and he appealed a total of 51 decisions to the Information Commissioner. The Commissioner also decided the requests were frivolous and vexatious and upheld the decision by RTÉ.

There is an onus on the organisation to assist you, but there is also an onus on you to be reasonable – not to the point where you limit the scope of what you actually want, but there is clearly no point in spreading a request so wide or making so many requests that they are all shot down at the first hurdle.

It is often the case that an FOI officer will contact you and ask, 'is there something specific you want?' Or, 'can we narrow down your request?' This is part of the organisation's duty to try to assist you to get the records you seek, and narrowing down the request is sometimes a feature of this process. Maybe this can be done or maybe it cannot.

It really is up to you to decide if you want to continue with a trawl or if you want to narrow the scope of your request. Both have inherent risks and benefits. Risks include the possibility that if you narrow the scope of your request too much, some key records may not be released because they now fall outside the remit of the revised request. And there are also risks if you do not change the scope of the original request because it may well be rejected as it is too vague for the organisation to deal with. The other possibility is that they could come back and say it will cost several hundred or indeed several thousand euro to give you the records you seek.

Such potential bills can be appealed to the Information Commissioner and can be done without having to pay the €150.00 fee. Section 47 of the Act sets out the requirements for charging fees but notes they can be waived if the issue is of 'national importance' (which is probably more of interest to journalists), but it also states that if the fee would be less than the cost of collecting and processing it, then the charge can be waived.

And remember, you can and should make a 'trawling' request if you feel it is the only way to obtain the records you want. It is up to the organisation to prove that your request would cause significant disruption to their regular workload or that it is frivolous.

Indeed, sometimes such trawls are the only way to get the records you seek and even if the organisation rejects your request, the Information Commissioner's office may or may not agree with them. There is also the possibility that the Commissioner's office may be able to find a compromise that suits all sides.

It's obvious but important to point out that you need to put your contact details on the request such as name and address. It is also a good idea to put a contact phone number and/or an e-mail address on the request. This simply speeds up the process of contacting you if the organisation wants to get in touch to discuss an aspect of the request.

For example, a State body might want to get in touch with you promptly if you submit a request but it does not have the records you want. There are several possible outcomes if this happens. The organisation can transfer your request to another body that does have them – as long as this second body is subject to the Act – and let them handle your request. Alternatively, they may simply write back to you with your €15.00 and say your request has nothing to do with them. If that happens and they do not advise who would have the records you seek then simply contact them and ask. If they know, they are supposed to advise and assist you.

But presuming your request has been sent to the correct organisation the clock starts running for them once the request and fee have been received because the Act imposes time limits on when a requestor should receive a reply.

Firstly, the organisation will acknowledge receipt of the request within ten working days of having received it. This is usually done in the form of a letter stating that the request was received on a specified day and, sometimes, when a full reply can be expected.

If you have not heard anything from the organisation a fortnight or so after sending a request then it is worth getting in touch with them to ensure that they have received it. If they have not, the only option is to send it in again. It can be sent in by post or hand delivered to the organisation, or if it relates just to personal information about you, just send in an email.

These acknowledgement letters are important as they usually set out your rights under the Act, such as the rights of appeal.

From the date of receiving the request, under Section 8 of the Act, the organisation has twenty working days to establish if they have the information being sought and, if so, to decide whether to release all of it, some of it or none of it. Frequently the organisation will contact you stating that they are extending the time to make a decision by a further twenty working days. The Act allows them to do this, and you need to bear in mind that in many organisations the FOI officer usually has other duties as well and your request is most likely one of many they are handling.

It is not part of their job to go rummaging around the organisation looking for records relating to your request. Typically, the FOI officer will contact the relevant section or sections asking them if they have the information being sought, and if so to come back to them with a list of what records they hold relating to the request.

When an FOI request is complex or controversial, it is usual for the organisation to take some time to process it – well beyond the initial twenty days set out in the Act. The FOI officer dealing with the request will gather a list of the records that it covers, but will also get opinions from those who work with these records as to their suitability for release or not.

Regularly other organisations which would have an interest in these records are consulted to get their views about whether they should be released. The Act does not say this should happen, but the Central Policy Unit from the Department of Finance has instructed FOI officers that 'good administrative practice would suggest' that these 'third parties' are informed of the request and, where possible, consulted. The CPU Notice 20 states that doing this would allow the decision maker the opportunity to inform themselves of all 'relevant factors' before making a decision. Somewhat alarmingly, the Notice goes on to state that this includes 'the appropriateness of the Act's exemptions' and lists a number of sections which were amended 'to provide explicit protection for records in which other public bodies have a significant interest'.

If the request seeks information provided by, or relating to, bodies outside of FOI, such as individuals or businesses who, for example, submitted a tender, then they too will be contacted to get their views on whether the information should be released or withheld. Their views can be important, but it does not necessarily mean that the deciding officer will go along with them.

If your request involves records dealing with international affairs, then the likelihood of encountering this negative approach to FOI is even greater. In the Central Policy Unit Notice 18, decision makers are made aware:

> '. . . of the damage that might be done to Ireland's international relations if public bodies in Ireland (and Government Departments in particular) are seen to be overly relaxed in releasing material . . . which could directly or

indirectly disclose details of the non-public positions and
views of a foreign authority.'

The notice spends five words outlining the core principle of FOI
– to provide access 'to the greatest extent possible' – before outlining in detail, over several pages, the various reasons a decision
maker could cite to refuse to release records. This is not just an
overly cautious approach – it indicates a fundamentally negative
approach to FOI.

These issues come into play once the FOI officer has received
back from the section or various sections of the organisation a list
of records covered by the FOI request. The matter is then discussed
among those involved in the relevant areas and a decision made to
release all, some or none of the records sought.

If it comes to light that some part of a record is held by the organisation which received the FOI request, but that a second body
also holds other parts of the record, then the organisation which
received the request will only process the portion in relation to the
record it holds. However, they should also inform you of the identity of the other organisation or organisations that hold the other
parts of the record. It is then up to you to make further applications
to these other bodies seeking the records they hold.

Depending on the records being sought, it may be relatively
straightforward for the organisation to decide to either grant access
in full, in part or to refuse to release the documents entirely. The
FOI officer will usually write to you stating that they have a number
of records relating to your request and, depending on how many
there are, may not seek a fee but instead just enclose the records.

But sometimes the organisation requests a fee for search and retrieval, as well as for copying the original records. The clock stops
on your request once the organisation has issued a letter requesting
payment, and only resumes again once they have either received

the full payment or an agreed deposit, for example if the fees charged are over €40.00.

The search and retrieval fee is €20.95 per hour, the charge for photocopying is four cent per page while a CD is €10.16. These fees are generally not charged if the request relates to personal information unless there are a lot of records involved. It has been known for organisations to seek hundreds of euro in such fees, particularly under the search and retrieval heading. In most cases the charges are genuinely incurred when dealing with the FOI request, but remember that just because a requestor pays out several hundred euro doesn't mean the records will contain what they hoped.

It is also worth noting that having paid over the money and received the records it is possible to argue that there was an overriding issue of national importance in the records being released and that all fees should be refunded. Obviously, this is somewhat easier for journalists to use as they can highlight the public interest impact of their story, but it has, on some occasions, been successful.

Having overcome the issues of fees and charges, several possible outcomes of an FOI request still remain. The first is the complete release of all records sought. They usually come in the form of photocopies of the original report or relevant documents. However, depending on what was actually sought, the records could be given on a computer disc or you could even be invited into the organisation to inspect the records sought or be given an opportunity to hear or view them (if it is audio visual form), or any combination of these. The records from the organisation are always accompanied with a covering letter, which is important because it usually contains a list or schedule of all the records relating to the request which have been found within the organisation.

The second possible outcome is that the requestor receives some of the records sought. That could take the form of releasing copies of all the records but with names, sentences, paragraphs or even several pages blocked out or redacted. The other form this could take is to entirely remove records or certain chapters and release what remains. Once again, the schedule or list of documents is important here. It should give a very brief description of every record that came under the remit of the Freedom of Information request, and then state whether it is being released in full, in part or not at all. The schedule should also state what section of the Act is being used to prevent release of the records.

The third possible outcome is that the request will be refused in its entirety. Once again, the schedule is crucial as it should list all documents held by the organisation but, just like when partially releasing records, the organisation has to state clearly under what section or sections of the Act they are refusing to release the information. It is not uncommon for one record to be protected by several different sections of the Act.

The fourth possible outcome is that the requestor never hears anything for the organisation following the acknowledgement letter. In that case the Act assumes the request is being denied and the requestor should then write to the organisation stating they wish to appeal the decision to refuse their request. These so-called Section 41 appeals do not attract a fee and instead the requestor simply contacts the organisation stating they want to appeal the refusal. If that too is ignored or not answered, then the only option is to appeal the 'non-decision' to the Information Commissioner.

The fifth possible outcome is that someone from the organisation will contact the requestor and see whether they can meet the request without going through the Freedom of Information Act. This benefits the organisation as it is often simpler and quicker to deal with, and can suit the requestor in that they may get the records they seek a lot quicker than they would under FOI. Of course, there is a risk that they won't receive all the records being sought, but that assumes the official they are dealing with has set out to pull a fast one, which in my view would very rarely happen.

Having got the information – what can be done with it? Well, the answer is pretty much anything as long as it is legal. Once again, it may seem obvious but the most important thing to do with the record or records you receive is to read them carefully – very carefully.

The schedule which accompanies the released documents usually has a brief description of what each record is about, such as an email from 'Mr. X to Ms. Y' or 'minutes of meeting dated 12th March'. If you receive a lot or records it is often worth ensuring you read them in chronological order to get a better understanding of the process that went on within the organisation – what people knew and said and when they knew and said it.

Usually the records come without any explanation – it is up to you to understand what they reveal. Since you sought these documents it is likely you will know at least something about their likely content. Still, you may need to spend a lot of time reading and re-reading any documents you get under FOI. There will be no high-lighted section saying 'this is the bit you're looking for', or 'this is the newsworthy bit', so it is up to you to understand what they contain. If there are a lot of records, it might also be worth summarising what each record says to get a 'bird's eye' view of the way the matter has been processed and discussed within an organisation.

Particularly with minutes of meetings, e-mails or letters, look out for who was in attendance or who was in contact with whom. It is important also to keep an eye on the dates of records. They obviously show when an organisation or individual was discussing an issue, and it often happens long before the matter enters the public arena. Dates also make it possible to track when an organisation became aware of a certain issue, for example, and when it decided to do something about it.

If, having read the records several times, you are confused about part or all of what was released, you could contact the FOI officer or the official directly involved (if identified) to try to clarify the issues. Generally, people will assist as much as possible, but remember they are not under any obligation to do so. The Freedom of Information Act allows access to records, but not to the knowledge those involved in creating them actually have.

It is also important to note that there are legal issues surrounding FOI records. You do not have copyright of the records, nor is there any legal protection attached to State records released under FOI. So, for example, if there are libellous statements made in a record and you repeat them then you can be sued by the person libelled. Also, you cannot claim the information has been created by you because it clearly has not – but you can say it has been obtained by you and credit the organisation as the source.

One of the most important elements of the Act is that it allows people access to personal information about them and held by a State body. Under Section 17 of the Act, people can seek and correct personal information if the information is 'incomplete, incorrect or misleading'. The Data Protection Act confers similar rights on an individual as well.

If you make a request and obtain records which you feel are inaccurate there is a procedure in place to change the official record. Firstly, you must write to the body which has the record, identify the record you want changed, identify the change you want and, crucially, provide information to back up the request. It is not enough to say, 'I want this changed' – you must be able to back up the contention that the official record is wrong or incomplete. You can make such a request in relation to personal information held about you or, if a parent or guardian, on behalf of a child or someone with a disability.

If the organisation accepts that their records are inaccurate or incomplete, they can alter the record, add a statement to the record to ensure that it becomes accurate or remove the incorrect information.

The official in the organisation dealing with the request will firstly consider the information supplied to back up the claim that the original record is inaccurate or incomplete. They may also discuss the issue with colleagues and view other files relating to the matter, for example, details of a particular scheme or plan. Once the official is happy that the original details are, on the balance of probabilities, incorrect they can go ahead and alter them.

If, however, the official decides that the original information was correct at the time the record was created, they do not have to alter it. They must inform the requestor within twenty days of the decision to refuse to amend the record and outline the appeals procedure. The matter must first be appealed within the organisation and then, if still not satisfied, the requestor can appeal the issue to the Information Commissioner.

Finally, one question that is regularly asked is how do you know that what the organisation is revealing under FOI is the whole story? The honest answer is, you do not. However, there is a legal obligation under the Act for the organisation to be open and honest, so it really is a matter of trust and most civil servants take their responsibilities very seriously. Given the fact that there are many sections in the Act which would allow an organisation to refuse to release information, it would not make sense to try to 'hide' records – especially if it could emerge later during an appeal.

It does happen that not all the records held by the organisation will be listed on the schedule that is issued in response to a request. In dealing with an application the body is supposed to contact all the sections within the organisation which are likely to hold the information being sought. It is always possible, however, that human error will result in a section not being contacted or not issuing a reply.

If you believe that the organisation has more information than they are listing on the schedule of records, it is a matter to be raised on appeal. Occasionally a body will uncover more records at this point, sometimes by themselves or sometimes having been pointed in a certain direction by the requestor. More often than not, however, additional records will not be found. It may be that the information being sought never actually existed or was simply never recorded, which often happens when people want to avoid their obligations under the Freedom of Information. Unfortunately, it is not as rare an occurrence as it should be.

4

Dealing with Refusals

ONCE IN A CONVERSATION WITH AN FOI officer about a request which had been rejected entirely, he told me that part of it had been legitimately refused . . . the unspoken inference being that the remainder of my request had been illegitimately refused.

There was no doubt that was his view, but it may not have been the view of the actual civil servant who decided what should and should not be released. Some would believe releasing certain records could have a damaging effect – however give the same document to another officer and they may draw a completely different conclusion.

There are many different sections of the Act that offer a range of measures to prevent records being released. Some of these are clearly defined, such as Cabinet documents, but many others are more subjective especially when it comes to a 'public interest test', that is, would the public interest best be served by releasing a record. Usually, in my experience, organisations decide that the public interest is best served by not releasing the information.

The figures, it seems, would back up the view that the culture of secrecy and refusal is alive and well within the civil service, but there are signs that perhaps it is beginning to change. According to figures from the Information Commissioner, the civil service is less likely to grant full release to records than other public bodies. For example, in 2010, just 41 per cent of requests to Government departments were granted in full – the lowest of any group under FOI – although this was a marginal increase on the 39 per cent the year before and 36 per cent in 2008. Unsurprisingly, these departments also had the highest refusal rate at 15 per cent. Thirty per cent were part granted, that is, had some parts of the records removed or redacted.

This poor release rate compares to an impressive 71 per cent of all requests to the HSE being granted in full and 76 per cent in the voluntary hospital, mental health and related services sector (although it must be pointed out that most of these requests are likely to be for personal information). Third level institutions and local authorities granted full access to records in 57 per cent of requests.

Overall, 60 per cent of requests for information are granted full access, 19 per cent are given partial access and 11 per cent are refused completely. One per cent of requests are transferred to another body while nine per cent are marked 'withdrawn/handled outside of FOI'.

Like all Acts around the world, the Irish version offers the State strong and clear powers to protect itself from being forced to release documents which could do some genuine harm and which would not serve the good of the wider public. The problem is that these same sections also afford an organisation the power to refuse to release information that *would* be in the public interest to publish and which would cause no harm whatsoever.

There has been a growing instance of what can only be described as sneaky evasion of FOI by the State in recent years. What has happened is that when new powers are being conferred on a body which is subject to the Act, or just when a piece of legislation is being passed, a clause is inserted somewhere to exclude either some or all of the organisation's crucial functions from FOI.

For example, as noted earlier, when changes were made to the Health and Safety Authority legislation, the enforcement functions were removed from the scope of the Act, and it was the same story with the Land Registry and the Registry of Deeds, which are both now exempt from FOI as they're controlled by the Property Registration Authority – which is, unsurprisingly, outside the remit of the Act.

There is also a 'nuclear' option which exists in several sections of the Act, which is the possibility of Ministerial/Secretary General Certificates being issued. These certificates are only supposed to be used when a matter of serious importance is still being considered, or if releasing the information would do grave harm. There is no appeal when a certificate is issued. The Information Commission is legally unable to examine whether the certificate is issued properly or not. It is only when the Minister or Secretary General decides that the certificate does not need to be renewed that the information can then be released.

In relation to appeals to the Information Commissioner, in most cases the figures show that overall State bodies have little to fear from such an appeal – as long as they've applied the Act correctly. According to the 2010 annual report by the Commissioner, in 29 per cent of cases the original decision to refuse or limit the release of records was affirmed on appeal. That seem highs and it is in fact a slight worsening of the situation. The previous year 32 per cent of original decisions were upheld, while in 2008 the figure was 31 per cent. This shows that of the cases taken to the Commissioner for appeal, she is finding that more and more of the decisions to refuse access to records are not in accordance with the Act.

Similarly, the number of cases where the original decision is annulled has shown a remarkable rise. In 2008 it happened in just four per cent of cases; in 2009 it was just two per cent of cases; but in 2010 the figure had risen significantly to seven per cent.

In 28 per cent of cases in 2010 a settlement was found between the requestor and the public body. That's a rise from 21 per cent in 2009 and 2008, and shows that more and more cases are being resolved by means of compromise. It can also mean that the public body has agreed to release all the information sought without having to go as far as getting a formal decision by the Commissioner. This would often happen when the public body would be told during consultations that the Commissioner's office is likely to allow some or all of the appeal against their original decision to refuse.

It is also interesting to note that the number of appeals withdrawn from the Commissioner has dropped to 26 per cent in 2010, down from 36 per cent the year before. This shows that there is less of a willingness to give up or settle an appeal – a decision has to be reached.

Overall, while the figures show that the chances of overturning an original decision are not high, it does happen. It is, statistically speaking, far more likely that a settlement will be reached which means some information may be released.

There is no doubt, looking at the Commissioner's annual reports and a grant rate of only 41 per cent, that the ideas of openness and transparency have a long way to go before they are core elements of the civil service.

In comparison, the Health Service Executive granted 71 per cent of requests in full, part granted access in 14 per cent and refused eight per cent of requests. The HSE is, in fact, the subject of most FOI requests – 35 per cent of all requests were made to the Executive as compared to 33 per cent to Government Departments. The HSE West and HSE South received the most requests of any organisation in 2010, with the Department of Social Protection a long way off in third spot.

However, although the HSE received 35 per cent of all requests, the Executive was responsible for over half of all appeals to the Information Commission on the grounds that the request was not dealt with within the timeframe set out in the Act, so-called 'deemed refusals'. In these cases, if a request is not answered within the strict time limits (or not answered at all), the requestor can appeal to the Information Commissioner without having to pay the €150.00 fee.

It is clear that appeals are part and parcel of FOI and it's equally clear that requests to Government departments are far more likely to result in a full or part refusal. Appeals are inevitable, so be prepared. And remember that just because an organisation cites one or, more usually, several exemptions – that does not make their decision right. The only way to find out is to appeal the decision to the Information Commissioner and let an independent person decide.

Of course, in many cases that costs €150.00 and time. Depending on what is being sought, it could be well worth the money and effort, but that is very much up to the individual, the nature of the request and, unfortunately, the ability to find €150.00 to lodge the appeal. Remember too that a fee is not payable if the request relates to personal information about the requestor or, in some cases, about their family. And as noted previously, the fee is not payable either if the public body does not answer the request within the timeframe set out by the Act.

There are many measures within the Act to prevent the release of information that would cause damage to an individual, body or indeed the country. They are categorised into several sections:

o 'The harm test' – the deciding officer must consider if harm would be done before releasing or refusing to release documents.

o 'The public interest test' – many exemptions have such a test where the deciding officer considers whether to release or not would be in the public interest.

- o 'The class test' – where an entire class of documents are exempt.

- o 'Mandatory exemptions' – where the Act says the deciding officer must refuse to release certain documents such as Government records. The words 'shall refuse' feature in a number of sections . . . especially since the 2003 review of the Act.

- o 'Discretionary exemptions' – where the deciding officer has a choice to refuse or release . . . the phrase 'may refuse' appears in a number of sections.

- o 'Protection of third parties' – if an individual or a company has been given commercially sensitive or personal information this type of protection is aimed at preventing it being released under FOI.

- o 'Certificates' – if a document can be released under the Act but a Minister or a Secretary General of a department issues a certificate ordering the organisation not to release it. There is no appeal in this case.

Part 3 of the Act outlines most, but by no means all, of the sections under which access to records can be refused.

It must be borne in mind that in some cases the decision to refuse is correct and will be backed up by the Commissioner and the courts. But in other cases the decision may be wrong. An organisation or the deciding officer may simply refuse because they have an overly cautious approach to releasing information, or they may seek to protect their organisation from controversy.

It also can happen that an initial request that is refused is upheld on appeal, or it is part granted or fully granted on appeal to the Commissioner, but then the High Court or the Supreme Court overturns it all again. Freedom of Information is not a science; it is a law and, like all laws, it is all about interpretation.

> *When several newspapers sought information about the Leaving Certificate results the requests were refused initially and again on internal appeal by the Department of Education. The Information Commissioner overturned that decision and ordered the Department to release the data sought. The Department then went to the High Court and got the Commissioner's decision overturned.*

In other cases the organisation will write back to you and say they have no records relating to your request. This may be a surprise as you may believe they should have records relating to the issue. Remember, however, that the Act allows access to records that exist and that the organisation has control over. The body is not under any obligation to go chase records from another organisation nor are they obliged to create records. However, in some cases an organisation will create a record to compile information as a result of a request rather than give the raw data. An example of this is the cost of a politician's visit to a foreign country. It would be possible just to copy the receipts and send them off, but often the Department can provide a record which just details all of the information.

If they don't hold the information they can and should transfer the request to another body as long as that body is subject to FOI. If the organisation who received the original request is the one who should have the records but insists they do not exist, you will be so informed in a letter. You could then seek an internal review, but if that still turns up nothing you will need to consider an appeal to the Information Commissioner.

The Commissioner's office won't go into the organisation themselves to seek the records, but they will question staff in the body about the records, ask if they did ever exist, where they might be, who could have handled them and so on.

It does happen that records do appear once an appeal has been lodged and sometimes additional records do turn up. In the majority of cases the Commissioner finds that the records actually do not exist, or that while they may have existed at some stage they can no longer be found.

In 2009 a farmer made an application to the Department of Agriculture seeking the name of a person who had made a report concerning the farmer's spreading of slurry. The Commissioner's office was told by the Department of the steps it had taken to find records relating to the issue but could find none. The Commissioner upheld the Department's refusal on the grounds the records sought did not exist.

In another case a person sought access to records held by Naas Town Council relating to the transfer of lands. The Council released one record saying that was all they had. On appeal to the Information Commissioner, it emerged they had many more documents which were only then released to the requestor. As the Commissioner's office continued their investigation it became known that the Council had not included any documents held by their legal advisors on their behalf which were subject to FOI and most of which were subsequently released.

When the decision by the body is to limit or refuse to release records you must be told exactly why and, more importantly, what section of the Act is being used to refuse release. You must also be told about your rights to appeal the decision.

If you make the request and are told by the organisation that they will release all the records they hold there is obviously nothing to appeal. However, be aware that your response may have come from just one section of the organisation. There may be records in another part of the body that have not been considered. It is always worth reading in detail who and in what section of the organisation the documents relate to. If you believe that there could be other records in another part of the body, then contact the official who issued the FOI response and inform them. They may come back and say, 'no, that's everything', or they may come back and say, 'we found these additional records'. Either way, if you think there are more records within the organisation then you should inquire first and be prepared to appeal.

It is also common to release records with parts or sometimes the entire contents blacked out or redacted. When that happens, it can make the release of the document fairly pointless because only occasional words or sentences are legible. In that case you need to consider how significant are those omissions and deletions. Are the records that have been released sufficient for what you wanted in the first place? If they are, then there is little point in appealing a decision. It will cost you money (if it is a non-personal request) and could waste valuable time within an organisation when it is unnecessary.

In cases where your request has been rejected entirely, you should examine what sections of the Act are being cited to deny you access. Sometimes sections which allow limited grounds for appeal are cited, but that does not mean it is not worth appealing. In some cases the Information Commissioner will decide that the documents do not satisfy the criteria of that particular section and that the records should be released.

> *This happened in a case where a politician sought copies of minutes of meetings relating to an interdepartmental group on employment. The Department of the Taoiseach refused, saying they were part of a deliberative process and they were for Government use. The Commissioner examined them and found neither to be the case and ordered their release, albeit with some parts redacted.*

According to the Information Commissioner, Emily O'Reilly, the quality of decision making by bodies subject to FOI has deteriorated because of the movement of staff and lack of training. This has resulted in decisions being made to refuse when they should not, leaving an appeal to her office as the only way to get the records sought.

Before you get that far, however, there is a process to go through. First you have to seek an internal review, which usually costs €75.00. Then, if you're still not happy with the result, you have to fork out a further €150.00 to appeal that decision to the Information Commissioner – that's a total cost €240.00 which represents a considerable investment without any guarantee of a return.

The first step in the appeals process is the internal appeal which involves a total re-examination of your request. When you submit your appeal you will receive an acknowledgement letter which will inform you of the date a decision is due, who is making that decision and your rights to appeal that decision if you are not happy with the outcome. If you do not receive that acknowledgement letter, contact the body to make sure they've received your appeal.

As part of this internal review, a more senior official than the one who made the original decision will examine all the records you are seeking. They will then decide if the original decision is correct or not. Sometimes more records are released on appeal and it is possible the original decision could be completely reversed and all the records sought are released. That, however, is a very rare occurrence.

Under the Act, the organisation has twenty working days to carry out this review. The review will often go beyond that date, however, and usually the organisation will contact you to let you know this is happening. They are entitled to an extension of another twenty days.

If you do not hear from that body within the time limit you are entitled to appeal to the Information Commissioner without paying the €150.00 fee. You should, however, contact the person identified on the appeal acknowledgement letter and try to find out if they are making a decision and if so when that is likely to happen. If you do not get anywhere then proceed with an appeal to the Commissioner.

So how do you actually write an appeal? Wording an appeal internally or to the Information Commissioner is very much down to an individual approach. You can just say, 'I wish to appeal the decision not to release the records I want', or you can make out a longer argument about why the records should be released.

The most comprehensive way is to address each point the organisation made in refusing access and make a counter argument to each one, section by section. You should be focused in writing the letter – set out an argument why the organisation's refusal or decision to limit the release was wrong and address each point it made in its decision.

For example, in reply to your request the organisation might state that the records are exempt under Section 21(a) and Section 30(1)(a). This means the deciding officer has ruled that the records will not be released to you because they could prejudice the functions and negotiations of public bodies (Section 21) and they could prejudice research being carried out by the State (Section 30).

Both these sections state that the 'head' of the organisation 'may refuse' to grant the request, but of course that also means they could grant it too. Both sections also have 'public interest' clauses as well, so you will need to make an argument as to how the public interest is best served by releasing the documents. Public interest does not mean that many people would necessarily be interested, but that there is a common good for the public if the records are released.

There is no definition of 'public interest' in the Irish FOI Act, but there is in the version from Queensland. It states that 'the public interest is served by promoting open discussion of public affairs and enhancing government's accountability'. That's an excellent description and worth quoting in appeals where there is a public interest clause.

It is important to address the core of each section cited by the organisation and counter any arguments that releasing the records would cause harm. This could be done by simply making a statement outlining how you believe the decision is wrong or you could argue, if appropriate, that the records are not exempt under these sections at all.

It is always a good idea to include references to previous decisions by the Information Commissioner using similar sections which back up your case. The Commissioner's website has an excellent search engine where you simply enter the section of the Act you are looking for and you get a list of cases where decisions have been made relating to that section. Simply read through them, find one that is appropriate where the decision was to release and quote from that judgement.

Having received your request for an appeal, the reviewing official in the organisation may get in contact with you to see if a compromise can be reached, or to explain the difficulties they face in releasing the records you seek. They may also offer to release some documents – under or outside of FOI – or they may say the original decision must stand. It is up to you to consider any offer that is made and whether it would satisfy what you're seeking. Once a final decision is made on your appeal, you will be notified by the organisation about its outcome.

This process is similar to the one conducted internally by the organisation in that it is essentially a brand new look at the case in its entirety. The Commissioner's office won't have any preconceived ideas and will approach the appeal with the view that records must be released unless the organisation can prove that to do so would cause harm or be illegal. This is hugely important, as it puts the emphasis on the organisation to defend the decision not to release and to provide convincing arguments to the Commissioner's office as to why they were right to refuse.

This is the case in all except Section 17 cases. This covers personal information about you or a person you are responsible for that is held by the organisation and which you claim is incomplete, incorrect or misleading. In these cases it is up to you to prove to the public body that this is so, and similarly on appeal to the Information Commissioner. It is the one area where the onus is on the requestor to prove the decision by the public body is incorrect.

A man who attended Cork University Hospital for treatment to a leg wound in 1994 sought to have the words 'self-inflicted?' removed from his file. He argued successfully that, on the balance of probabilities, the doctor who recorded the words was incorrect.

> *A woman sought to amend records held by the Revenue Commissioners following a dispute between her and her husband on one side and the Revenue on the other. While her husband did make a settlement, she sought to amend the record via Section 17, specifically, her living expenses. Revenue refused saying there was no evidence to back up her claim. The Commissioner agreed and refused the appeal.*

So especially in Section 17 appeals it is necessary to be able to back up your claims that the information is incorrect, misleading or incomplete.

In drawing up an appeal to the Commissioner you should include all correspondence between you and the body from the initial request onwards. As with the internal appeal, background documents or newspaper cuttings which support your case should also be included. Judgements from other jurisdictions can also be quoted – particularly FOI decisions from the UK and Queensland in Australia. In addition, it is worth taking the time to think about what other arguments the organisation may make to refuse to release the records and draw up counter-arguments to submit in your appeal.

The obvious drawback to this type of detailed appeal is that it does take time to write and there is, of course, no guarantee that the Commissioner will rule in your favour. It is, nonetheless, probably the best way to appeal.

Once your appeal has been received by the Commissioner's office, it is assessed to see if it can be accepted, for example, whether it is within the timeframe, the fee is enclosed and so on. If it is accepted you will be notified in writing by the Commission.

A member of the Commissioner's staff will then be assigned to your case – but beware this can take many months depending on the backlog of cases in the Commissioner's office. The investigator appointed by the Commissioner to examine the appeal will look at the whole issue and not just rely on your submission. However, it does provide a good 'road map' for them. By law the State organisation has to present the records you've sought to the Commissioner's office for the investigator to inspect them. This will allow the inspector to draw up an independent view of whether the exemptions claimed by the body over the records are valid. Depending on what the investigator finds in the records, they may contact you and the organisation itself to see if an accommodation or agreement can be reached which would be mutually acceptable.

At any stage in your appeal you can make additional submissions to the Commissioner's office, highlighting, for example, new information that has come to light. However, it is important to remain focused when appealing a decision. The investigating officer is not overly interested in your background or your views on the organisation. What they are interested in is getting your views on the decision not to release the records you sought and why they should be released.

Later on the investigator may contact you and give their preliminary view on your appeal having examined the records sought and read submissions from both sides. This also could be part of the efforts to find a compromise.

It is important to take on board what the investigator says. They may indicate that they entirely support your view which means it is up to the organisation to try to convince them they are wrong. The investigator may say some records can be released but others cannot, or they may indicate that they will hold against you and dismiss your appeal entirely which means you then have to try to convince them they are wrong. This is not impossible, but it certainly will not be easy.

There are no definitive statistics available about the number of preliminary decisions which are changed or reversed entirely by the time it gets to a final decision, but it does happen. It is estimated that maybe in one in five cases the preliminary view changes by the time a final decision is made. This could be due to further submissions being made by either side, new information emerging or simply the Commissioner disagreeing with the preliminary view of the investigator.

It is worth noting that if you settle or withdraw a case before a final decision is reached, you will have the €150.00 fee returned to you. However, it is also important to note that if you wish to take High Court action in relation to your case, you will need the Commissioner to make a final determination on the matter.

Over the coming pages we'll go through the more common sections of the Act which a body can use to refuse access to records. Using this guide you will be able to quickly see the reason or reasons an organisation is citing to limit or refuse your request. There are also suggestions as to how to appeal each section.

It is important to remember that the appeals process is there to be used, and regardless of how you actually do it the key issue is to appeal when you feel it is necessary.

5

FOI, Section by Section

THIS CHAPTER LISTS THE SECTIONS of the Freedom of Information Act that are likely to feature in applications and appeals. When an organisation replies to an FOI request and either limits or refuses to release information, they will cite various sections of the Act as the reason for their decision. This chapter does not cover every single section of the Act which might be cited in a case – just the ones most likely to feature.

This section by section guide explains in straight-forward language what the organisation is saying and offers suggestions as to how to appeal such decisions.

Section 10

This section of the Act allows refusals for administrative reasons.

o Subsection 1(a) – an organisation may refuse a request if the record sought does not exist or 'cannot be found after all reasonable steps' have been taken to find it.

o Subsection 1(b) – refusal on the grounds the request does not contain sufficient details to allow the organisation to identify the records being sought.

o Subsection 1(c) – refusal on the grounds that to meet the request would require the retrieval and examination of so many records that it would cause 'a substantial and unreasonable interference' with the work of the organisation.

o   Subsection 1(d) – refusal if, by law, a record has to be published anyway within twelve weeks of your request.

o   Subsection 1(e) – refusal if the request is, in the opinion of the deciding officer, 'frivolous or vexatious' or forms part of a pattern of 'manifestly unreasonable requests' from the same person or persons acting together.

o   Subsection 1(f) – refusal if the fees sought have not been paid.

o   Subsection 2 – a deciding officer can only refuse after they have helped or offered to help the person change their request so it can be processed.

Section 10 refusals are reasonably common – usually on the grounds that the records do not exist or cannot be found.

It is also worth nothing that while many people may think or presume that certain records do exist, in reality they may not. There is no provision in the Act to force an organisation to create a record which someone believes they should have. The Act only applies to records which already exist – whether the requestor believes that to be sufficient or not is irrelevant. Occasionally, an organisation will create a record to fulfil an FOI request such as the compilation of statistics. It is easier to meet a request for that kind of information rather than release record after record with just the raw data.

Remember also that this Act allows for access to records – not information! To give an example, if a requestor seeks statistical information from a certain body, say how many medical procedures have been carried out in a certain hospital unit over the last five years, the hospital may have the day-to-day figures but not the statistics done over a five-year period. The hospital could argue that to compile the figures as requested would cause unwarranted interference with its usual work, but the requestor could then seek the raw information themselves and spend time compiling the figures as they want.

Almost invariably the decisions which cite Section 10(1)(a) are upheld by the Commissioner because the records do not exist. The Commissioner's job is not to go into the organisation and search for themselves, but instead to examine whether the organisation had taken all reasonable steps to search and retrieve the records sought. If the Commissioner is satisfied that they have done that and nothing was found, then that is pretty much the end of the matter. However, it is not unusual for records to come to light during an appeal to the Commissioner's office. It is also important to note that under this section, the organisation does not need to physically have the records – they must just be in a position to control them. For example, the records could be in an archive somewhere else or in an office belonging to an advisor or legal company. If they were created by or on behalf of the organisation, then they are deemed to be under their control.

In September 2009, a woman submitted an FOI application to the Midland Regional Hospital in Tullamore seeking a copy of the birth register which would give details of her birth. As both parents were dead this was her only avenue. However, despite extensive searches the hospital could not find the specific birth register needed. On appeal to the Information Commissioner, the hospital outlined the searches it had undertaken and it was accepted that the record could not be found. The woman's FOI request was therefore rejected under Section 10(1)(a).

If an organisation has a problem identifying what exactly you are looking for, or if it feels your request is so broad that it would disrupt their normal day-to day work, they can refuse to release under subsections (b) and (c). The best way to avoid this is to communicate with the deciding officer and try to reach an accommodation. Certainly it should be possible to identify what records you are looking for but subsection (c) may prove trickier. If you feel you cannot narrow the scope of the request, or if it's your belief that the body is using this section to avoid releasing information, then the only option is to refuse to budge and pursue an internal appeal. It will, almost certainly, end up with the Information Commissioner. As always, there is no guarantee that you will succeed but you can of course submit another request if you do not. This second time, however, you will have to be more precise because the body can rely on the previous ruling by the Commissioner to refuse your request straight away.

For an organisation to claim that to release the records being sought would cause 'a substantial and unreasonable interference' with their work (subsection c), they have to be able to prove to the Information Commissioner that compiling the information sought would severely impact on their day to day operation. If the Commissioner accepts that, and most recent judgements have gone that way, then the appeal will not succeed.

Refusal under Subsection (e), that is, frivolous or vexatious requests, is one not taken lightly by the deciding officer and usually follows a pattern of requests which target an individual or part of an organisation – usually by a person or persons holding a grudge.

Of course, the definition of a frivolous or vexatious request is very much the key here and this is the only area in the Act where a deciding officer can consider issues like the intent of the person making the request. In previous decisions, the Information Commissioner has ruled that issues such as the number of requests, their scope and nature, the purpose of the requests, their sequencing and, crucially, the intent of the person making the request all can be considered in making a decision on whether a request is frivolous or vexatious.

In a five month period of 2006, one former student was responsible for nearly 37 per cent of all appeals to the Information Commissioner's office as part of a long-running row with Trinity College, Dublin. He had submitted 107 requests to the university over the same period. The Information Commission ruled that the former student was, by the sheer volume of requests, engaged in an abuse of the process and that they were frivolous and vexatious.

Section 11

This section allows an organisation to defer giving access to records as well as to refuse. Under this Section, a deciding officer can decide to give you records but only after a certain time or after their publication.

o   Subsection 1(a) – refusal if a record was prepared 'solely' for the information of either the Dáil or Seanad, or an Oireachtas committee, and will be provided to them within 'a reasonable time'.

o   Subsection 1(b) – refusal if the records contain factual information, is a report of the efficiency or effectiveness of an organisation or is a scientific report or analysis *and* is due to the published shortly, the deciding officer can decide that it is not in the public interest to release the information before it is published.

o   Subsection 1(c) – refusal if the Minister responsible for the organisation decides to publish the information before it is released to the requestor. The Minister must publish the information within twenty-five working days of the FOI request being received.

If a request is being deferred under Section 11, the requestor will be told when the records will be made available and, as always, will be told of their rights to appeal.

Unusually, deferral under subsections 1(b) and (c) do not need to be appealed within the organisation but instead should be appealed directly to the Information Commissioner. Unfortunately, given the length of time it takes to get a decision from the Commissioner's office due to the backlog of cases, it is likely that the information will be published long before an appeal would be heard.

In the event that the records are not published within the timeframe, it's best to keep in contact with the organisation directly and remind them that the time period has expired and you are entitled to the records sought. They cannot seek further extensions *ad infinitum*. It is probably advisable to lodge an appeal with the Information Commissioner so at least the body knows you are determined to follow through on your request and that they will have to disclose the information at some stage.

Section 13

This section allows for parts of records to be withheld by the organisation.

o Subsection 1 – if a record should be released but contains a paragraph or pages that should not be released, then this section allows the organisation to redact that information and then release what remains.

o Subsection 2 – if releasing a record with so much removed from it that it would give a misleading impression then the whole document can be refused in its entirely under this subsection.

o Subsection 3 – a requestor must be told that part of the record has been removed and what they get is not the complete version. The organisation should also specify the nature of the material they have removed from the records.

This section gives authorisation to the body to remove parts of documents before release. Records released frequently have words, sentences, paragraphs or even entire pages redacted – or blanked out. It's not unusual to have a request 'granted' (minutes of a meetings, for example) but then only receive pages and pages of blanked out records with just occasional words or sentences left in. This frequently renders the documents useless, but it allows the organisation to keep down the number of FOI requests they refuse which looks good for them.

Subsection 2 allows the organisation to actually refuse to release the whole record if, having removed all the material the deciding officer feels they can remove, what is left would give an erroneous view of what the original record actually said.

The key point in Subsection 3 is that the organisation should tell you what type of information they have removed from the records. Obviously, they are not going to tell you exactly what was removed because that would then defeat the purpose of removing it in the first place, but you should be able to get a sense of what was taken out.

The usual argument made on internal appeal or an appeal to the Information Commissioner regarding this section is that the removal of the information has limited the scope of the requestor to understand or make sense of the records that have been released. It could be argued that the organisation may be adopting an overly cautious approach and that they have taken out more than they should have. Perhaps there has been public discussion of the issues surrounding the records you have sought which could back up your case. The obvious weakness with this argument is that unless you know what has been removed, you cannot be sure that the body has been over cautious. Nonetheless, it is often a valid argument because the official deciding the appeal will have full access to the original records. On appeal to the Information Commissioner, her office too will have access to the full range of documents and so can offer an independent view of the original decision.

In 2006 a student sought copies of his third year English exams and the identity of staff of the university who had claimed he had upset, abused or libelled. The exam papers had notes written by staff on them and the college refused to release on the grounds that the staff concerned were fearful for their safety because of threats from the student. This was appealed to the Information Commissioner. In her decision, the Commissioner noted that Section 13 gave the college the power to redact the names of the staff involved but added that verbal abuse would not necessarily be enough to invoke Section 23 which would allow a refusal as a result of fears for safety. However, the Commissioner said that the student's behaviour went beyond just verbal abuse. She ordered the release of several documents but agreed with the College to withhold information which would identify staff.

Section 17

This Section allows for amendments to be made to records relating to personal information. If information is held by a public body that it is incorrect or incomplete, people can make applications under this Section to ensure that the records are changed and kept up-to-date.

- o Subsection 1 – if personal information is incomplete, incorrect or misleading, and the person to whom the information relates wishes, a public body can:
  - Change the record to make the information complete or correct
  - Add information to the record stating that the public body accepts their information is incomplete or incorrect
  - Just delete the inaccurate or incomplete information.

- o Subsection 2 – when a person is making an application to change personal information they should:
  - Specify the record that contains the mistakes and what amendments they want
  - Include relevant information to back up their claims that the original document is wrong.

- o Subsection 3 – the deciding officer has four weeks from the date of receiving the application to decide whether to grant the request for changes or refuse them and must let the requestor know.

- o Subsection 4(a) – if the decision is to refuse then the deciding officer must:
  - attach to the original record which the person wanted changed their request for the information on it to be changed
  - include in his letter stating that he is refusing the application and include how to go about making an appeal.

- o Subsection 4(b) – a deciding officer does not have to attach the request for change to the original document if it is defamatory or unnecessarily voluminous.

o   Subsection 5 – when a record has been changed the public body must take 'all reasonable steps' to notify others of the change if they received the record in the previous twelve months. These are:

- any person who was allowed access to the record under FOI and,
- any public body which was given a copy of the record.

o   Subsection 6 – gives the Minister for Finance the power to make regulations that:

- a parent or guardian of an individual can make a request on behalf a person if that person belongs to a category specified in the regulation
- if a person is dead then a member of a group set out in the regulation (for example, family members) can make an application.

This section is one of the most important sections for people seeking personal information. It sets out the entitlements people have to make corrections to official records held by a public body, but only if that organisation is satisfied that the information is wrong. It is up to the requestor to prove that it is. However, this is not a section that can be used, for example, to get the results of a test re-examined and a higher award given.

It is obvious that the requestor has to have obtained a copy of the record in the first place to see that there are mistakes on it and then request them to be changed. As this relates to personal information, remember too that you do not have to pay a fee to make this application – or to seek the original records in the first place.

Subsection 1 says that when a person makes an application to have personal information changed, they can do it in writing or 'in such other form as may be determined'. That could be a simple phone call but it is always best to do this type of request via 'permanent' record such as e-mail or paper. If the deciding officer agrees then they can amend the record by adding or removing the incorrect information and/or adding a statement to the original record where they acknowledge the original information was wrong in some way.

Subsection 2 clearly sets out the grounds that you have to make before an application under this Section can be considered. The phrase 'as far as is practicable' means you do not have to know the exact record and there is an onus on the public body to help you. However, you will have to supply appropriate information to back up your claim that the original record is wrong. It simply will not suffice to say that it is incorrect and that it must be changed (unless the record says you are dead and clearly you are not).

Subsection 3 allows the deciding officer four weeks to consider the application and make a decision whether to grant or refuse the request. However, under Subsection 4, if the decision is to refuse the public body must attach to the original record your request for it to be changed. If that is not possible then they must attach a note saying you wanted it changed. They must also advise you of your rights of appeal. But if the amendment you're seeking is, in the opinion of the decision maker, either defamatory or simply too large, then they do not have to attach it to the original record.

If the decision is made to change the record, then under Subsection 5, the public body has to 'take all reasonable steps' to notify anyone who, in the last twelve months, was granted access to this record through the Freedom of Information Act, or any other public body who was given a copy of the original information.

Subsection 6 gives the Minister for Finance the power to introduce regulations which allow parents, guardians or, if a person is dead, other close family members to make applications on behalf of a person.

Many appeals under this section to the Information Commissioner have related to people seeking to change exam results or assessments, or to get information changed on files held by the HSE or another State body. Only a handful have met with any success as the requirements under this section put the onus on the requestor to prove that the information on the file is incorrect, incomplete or misleading. That is easier said than done. You must put forward strong evidence to back up your request for change. The Commissioner's office will work on the basis of the 'balance of probabilities', that is, which version of the facts is more likely to be correct in the view of the Commissioner's investigative staff.

Having been turned down for promotion, a wildlife ranger employed by the Department of Arts, Heritage, Gaeltacht and the Islands sought to have his personal records amended, including negative remarks on three performance reports. The Information Commissioner said that much of the evidence put forward by the ranger in seeking to get the performance reports changed was anecdotal as was the evidence put forward by the Department. The Commissioner ruled that it would not be appropriate to accept one person's version of events to the detriment of another unless there was compelling evidence obliging him to do so. While all three reports were flawed, the requester had not presented sufficient evidence to persuade the Commissioner that the ratings awarded in the reports was 'incomplete, incorrect or misleading' as required under this section of the Act.

There is also the issue of what exactly is personal information. In an interesting decision relating to a Section 17 application, the Commissioner ruled that records are personal only when they contain information which would be considered private. In essence, just because the record may have information about you, that does not make it personal and therefore liable to change under Section 17.

To be subject to change the information must be of a type that would be private and not generally known to others. If a record contains opinions about a person's actions while doing their job, the Commissioner ruled that these were not personal records as they do not reveal anything private about the individual and so would not be treated as confidential.

> *In October 2000 an official working for a Government department sought to change several records in which he was named. The Department refused and the matter was appealed to the Information Commissioner. She decided that the records are not personal under the Act as, although they contained views and assessments of the official's work, they did not reveal anything private about the official and therefore were not personal records.*

And then there is the issue of when a record is incomplete. In this regard there is a subtle nuance in this section that the Information Commission has highlighted on a number of occasions. If, having examined a personal file or record you believe that it is somewhat unfair and that there should be more information on it, such as favourable comments made by a senior official, there is no guarantee that an application under Section 17 to have that included will succeed.

The Commissioner has ruled that just because a record does not contain everything someone would like to see in it, that does not necessarily make the entire record incomplete. The Commissioner's view is that whatever the actual information is in the record itself must be wrong or incomplete to allow a change to be made. You may want more information included, but that is not necessarily possible under this section.

Many of the records that people have sought to change have included opinions by others about the requestor. Getting an opinion changed is not easy as the Commissioner has set the bar pretty high in that regard. To succeed, the requestor must be able to prove convincingly that the original view was flawed due to total inadequacy of the factual information upon which it was based, or that there was bias or ill will towards the requestor. The other ground for getting an opinion changed would be if the person who issued the opinion showed lack of balance or did not have the sufficient experience to make such a finding.

It's something of a similar story for those seeking to get marks or grades altered via Section 17. The Commissioner's view is that the Office would be slow to change them, or indeed comments made by an interview board, unless there is strong evidence to back up claims that the decisions or comments were flawed.

There have been several appeals to the Commissioner in cases where people who felt they did not receive an appropriate mark in an exam made applications under this Section to have their exam paper effectively looked at again.

In May 2007, an official with the Revenue Commissioners sat an exam in Revenue Law at the University of Limerick. However, he felt he deserved an A1 grade. The university re-examined it and improved it by one grade to a B2. The official took the matter to the Information Commissioner who found irregularities in the way the University handled their contact with the Commissioner. However, despite this, she ruled that Sections 17 and 18 were not 'appropriate mechanisms for challenging the outcome' of a marking scheme and dismissed his appeal.

> *A student from University College Dublin was unsatisfied with his result from an exam he sat in 2002. His father, who is an expert in the same area, looked at his son's paper and said he should have received a higher mark. The Internal Examinations Appeal Committee also looked at the paper and gave him a higher mark but not as high as his father. The student appealed to the Information Commissioner who ruled that the Committee was the proper forum for appealing the marking of exam papers and rejected his appeal.*

So while accessing personal information is an integral part of the Freedom of Information Act, we have seen that getting information changed is not that easy. You may disagree with something on a report, but unless there is the evidence to back your view you will not succeed. There remains, however, the fact that even if your request for change is not accepted your concerns and original request will be attached to the record so at least anyone who looks at it in the future will be able to see that you disagreed with the record.

Section 18

This section allows people the right to obtain information regarding the actions of a public body which impacts on them.

o Subsection 1 – after an application is made to the public body by a person affected by that action and who has a material interest in the issue, the public body must issue a statement to that person within four weeks
  • which will give the reasons for the action by the public body
  • and any findings of facts made for the purposes of the action.

o Subsection 2 – a person will not, however, through this Section, be able to

- get information from an exempt record (such as cabinet minutes)
- be told if a record exits or not if the Act says they should not be told.

o Subsection 3 – in the following cases, people cannot use Section 18 to get information about:
  - a decision of the Civil Service Commissioners not to recommend a person for a job
  - a decision by the Local Appointments Commissioner not to recommend a person for a job
  - but only if the head of the organisation involves believes that to do so would prejudice the effectiveness of the candidate selection process.

o Subsection 4 – if the organisation decides not to issue the statement based on either subsection 2 or 3 they must inform the requestor within four weeks.

o Subsection 5 – 'material interest' is defined as the actions of a public body which result in the granting or withholding of a benefit to a person or to a group of people.

o Subsection 5(A) – the Minister for Finance has the power to make regulations which:
  - grant parents or guardians of a person the right to make an application on their behalf
  - where a person is dead, the right to make an application by another close family member.

o Subsection 6 – gives definitions to various parts of this subsection like 'act' is a decision of the public body and 'benefit' includes:
  - any advantage to the person
  - consequences of the action by the public body

- the avoidance of loss, liability, penalty, forfeiture, punishment or other disadvantage.

This Section allows people who have been affected by a decision of a public body, for example not to get a promotion, a grant or an allowance, to seek a statement from the body which would explain why they did not get it.

Under subsection 1 a person is entitled to a statement outlining the reasons from a public body for the way it acted. That statement should be clear and understandable.

However, subsection 2 states that this requirement does not extend to records which are exempt from release under FOI. This could include a wide range of records such as Cabinet or other documents which cannot be released, such as those from the Commissioner's office or the Attorney General's office which deal with anything other than the administration of those offices.

Those making requests for a statement relating to why they did not get a job or promotion under the Civil Service Commissioners or the Local Appointments Commissioners may not get such a statement, but only if the deciding officer believes that if they did it would harm the selection process. If a request is refused on these grounds, it is open to you in an appeal to the Information Commissioner to argue that releasing a statement would not harm the selection process. However if you succeed it will only allow for a statement to be issued by the body – it will not allow for a rehearing of interviews or anything like that.

Subsection 4 merely states that if the deciding officer decides not to release a statement they have to tell you within four weeks.

Subsection 5 is crucial as it states exactly what a 'material interest' is. If the deciding officer rules that you have no material interest in the matter then they do not have to release a statement detailing why the organisation took the decision it did. To have a material interest you must either have received or been refused a benefit. Under this subsection you do not have to be the only person to have been affected. This subsection says that you could be one of a number of people 'which is significant size' and of which you are just one person who has been affected by the decision of the organisation. This subsection also gives the Minister for Finance the power to make regulations allowing those who are responsible for individuals who cannot make an application (such as children or people with an incapacity) the ability to make an application on their behalf.

Subsection 6 includes some important definitions such as what is an 'act' of a public body. It says that an 'act' means a decision which would result in a benefit to someone or some group. This benefit is defined as an advantage (such as a extra payment) but also includes issues like the consequence of that organisation's decision (such as the impact on a land-owner of rezoning land) or where a person avoids some sort of loss or punishment such as fines or forfeiture.

Overall, the success rate of appeals to the office of the Information Commissioner under Section 18 is very poor. Most people seemed to be of the view that taking such an appeal would allow for the original issue, such as a job interview, to be re-examined. Section 18 does not allow for that.

The appeal only relates to whether the public body issued a statement of reasons to the requestor which adequately and clearly explained how and why the decision was made. If it did then there are no real grounds for appeal to the Information Commission. However, if the statement is not adequate or cannot be clearly understood, then there are good grounds for an appeal. The statement itself should also identify the relevant criteria used by the organisation and the role each of them played in the decision it made.

However, according to rulings by the Information Commissioner, it does not have to clarify all the issues a requestor says are relevant.

> In October 2009, a member of staff at the Dublin Institute of Technology sought a statement of reasons from them regarding the selection process for a position in the Institute which he failed to get. In return he got a seven page statement. The matter ended up with the Information Commissioner who said the key factor in a statement of reason is that it should be easily understood but does not have to answer every single point raised by a person. The Commissioner said her role in this appeal is to ensure the statement is understandable. In this case she decided it was and so the appeal was rejected.

> In 2000, a farmer appealed to the Information Commissioner following a decision by the Department of Agriculture not to give him a statement of reasons in relation to dealings with officials regarding the Sheep Headage Scheme. The farmer claimed that they had failed to give him documents and made comments about him. There were four separate cases involved. Two of them related to his application and the Department had issued statements of reason regarding them. However, the other two cases related to the farmer's allegation they'd failed to give him full documentation and made comments about him. The Department refused to give a statement of reasons in these two cases.
>
> The Commissioner ordered the Department to re-issue the two statements but in a clearer form. However, in the two other cases, the Commissioner decided they did not have to. He said that a public body does not have to give reasons for every action of a member of staff, even if there was a case of maladministration involved.

Despite the cases above, there are occasions when a Section 18 appeal does succeed, though they are rare.

> *In 2005 the Department of Justice, Equality and Law Reform refused to grant a certificate of naturalisation to a man and refused then to provide a statement of reasons under Section 18. The Department argued that the decision was made at the absolute discretion of the Minister and so they did not have to issue a statement of reasons. However, the Commissioner disagreed and said there was no such exclusion from the FOI Act and ordered that a statement be issued by the Department.*

However, most other similar appeals are rejected by the Commissioner on various other grounds. So overall Section 18 appeals are tricky and are only worth taking if, having made a request for a statement of reasons, the reply was overly complicated or there was no reply at all. It is not worth the effort of making an appeal under this Section if you want to get a decision reversed – you will not succeed. This section only allows you access the reasons why a decision was made.

Section 19

This section allows for the protection of Government documents. Its scope was increased dramatically during the 2003 review and is frequently cited when seeking Departmental records.

o   Subsection 1 – under the original Act a deciding officer had some discretion whether to release or not, but that was changed from 'may refuse' to 'shall refuse' in the review.

o Subsection 1(a) – orders a refusal if a record has been or, or is to be, submitted to the Government by a Minister or the Attorney General and was created for that purpose.

o Subsection 1(aa) – orders a refusal if the record consists of a communication (for example, an e-mail or letter) between two or more members of the Government relating to Government business, or between two or more members of a group set up to consider an issue that is, or soon will be, discussed by the Government.

o Subsection 1(b) – orders a refusal if it is a record of Government business, but this does not apply to records on subjects where decisions have been announced by the Government.

o Subsection 1(c) – orders a refusal if the record contains information for a member of Government, the Attorney General, a Minister of State or the Secretary and Assistant Secretary to the Government which generally relates to Government business.

o Subsection 2(a) – orders that records which could show what was said at Government should not be released.

o Subsection 2(b) – records which do not relate to the published or announced decisions of the Government should not be released.

o Subsection 3 – states however that the exemptions listed in Subsection 1 do not apply if:
   • the record contains factual information relating to a decision that the Government has announced
   • if the record relates to Government decisions made 10 years ago
   • if the record relates to communications between Ministers was made 10 or more years ago.

o   Subsection 6 – contains several definitions such as a 'decision of
    the government includes the noting or approving of a record'
    and that a 'record' includes preliminary or other draft reports as
    well as finalised information.

As already noted, the definition of Government was dramatically expanded during the 2003 review. In the Act, Government was
defined as being the Cabinet, any committee consisting of at least
one of the following: members of the Government, the Attorney
General or Minister of State. But then it was expanded considerably
in 2003 and now includes a committee of officials (that is, civil servants, special advisors or anyone else they decide) appointed by the
Government to assist them on an issue. It also covers a committee
of officials that has been asked to report to the Government on a
topic, and any group which, on its creation, the Secretary General
to the Government decides should be covered by this section. The
scope of this is simply breathtaking and allows a vast range of work
to be exempt from release for ten years.

Subsection 2, which relates to records which reveal what was
said in Cabinet, is not subject to the ten-year limit. The Constitution bars such information being released ever, so regardless of
when the record was created, if it reveals who said something at
Cabinet then it will never be releasable under FOI.

Subsection 3 states that Government records created ten or
more years ago can be released, but it also allows for the release of
Government records which contain factual information, once the
Government decision based on these records has been announced.

Although there is a need for Government to be able to do some
of its business in confidence, Section 19 is, quite simply, a decade-
long blanket ban on finding out what goes on at Government. The
vast scope of this expanded section is simply to keep the public ig-
norant. It does not make for better government, as was argued

when the restrictions were announced. In fact, it is arguable the opposite is the case. With this 'cloak of invisibility' surrounding the Government, only a handful of politicians and senior civil servants know what's really going on and that's the way they want to keep it.

Making a case for the release of documents when Section 19 has been applied is, to say the least, difficult. Unlike other sections where there is discretion or a public interest test, there is nothing like that here. Although there are occasions that the Information Commissioner has decided that the Government Department has erred and that Section 19 does not cover the records a person seeks, there usually are a number of other sections which prevent their release anyway.

In making an argument on appeal, the only real case to make is that the Department has erred and that the records are not covered by Section 19. If you're seeking records relating to a Government decision that's already been announced, it is possible to argue that subsection 3(a) applies and that the information therefore can be released as it is permitted under the Act.

In 2005, John Burns from the Sunday Times *sought but was refused documents relating to the Government's decision relating to the decentralisation programme. The Department of Finance refused on a variety of grounds, including Section 19. In her decision the Information Commissioner ruled that some of the documents were exempt but others, including ones which had been refused under Section 19, should not have been exempt and she ordered their release.*

In 2007 the Commissioner became involved in an appeal where the Department of Finance had refused most of a request seeking records relating to the owning and running of Terminal 2 in Dublin Airport. The Department relied on several sections of the Act, including Section 19, and in almost all cases the Commissioner agreed.

Because of the wide scope of Section 19, appealing decisions where it has been cited are difficult and have a poor chance of success. However, that doesn't mean appeals should not be made. They should in all circumstances because it is only by doing this will awareness of the difficulties of Section 19 become more apparent to more people and there is always the hope that some decisions might go your way – but just don't get your hopes up too high!

Section 20

This section is designed to protect the deliberations of public bodies while internal discussions are continuing, so called 'thinking space'.

o Subsection 1 – the deciding officer may refuse to release records if they contain matters relating to the deliberative process, including opinions, advice, recommendations and results of consultations, for example. It is important to note the word 'may' in the first line as this means the deciding officers have discretion and will make an individual judgement on whether to release the records being sought.

o Subsection 1(A) – a Secretary General of a Government Department can issue a certificate which means records relating to that topic cannot be released. This is final and no appeal can be made against the issuing of such a certificate. This only applies to Government departments and other organisations like semi-state bodies cannot impose such certificates on themselves.

o Subsection 2 – the exemption does not cover records used or to be used to make recommendations or decisions; factual information; the reasons the organisation made a decision; any report or investigation into the performance, efficiency or effectiveness of the body; a report, study or scientific analysis commissioned for an organisation.

o Subsection 3 – if the decision maker decides that the public interest is best served by releasing records, then they can be published. This, however, does not extend to records which are covered by certificates issued under Subsection (1)(A).

This section is used by organisations regularly to prevent the release of documents relating to a deliberative process within the body. Different organisations have different interpretations of what such a process is or how long it can go on. Certificates are powerful tools available to Ministers and Secretaries General of Departments. Once issued, there is no internal appeal or appeal to the Information Commissioner and they remain in force until the Minister or Secretary General is 'satisfied that the deliberative processes concerned have ended'. However, there is no oversight to ensure that certificates are not kept in existence any longer than is necessary – it really is up to the person who signed them in the first place to decide when they want to revoke them.

Importantly, there are so-called 'harm' tests as well as a public interest clause in this section. This means that unlike Section 19, the deciding officer has a choice whether to refuse or to release.

To claim Section 20 exempts the body from releasing documents, other than the issuing of a certificate which requires no explanation, and the organisation must be able to prove to the Commissioner that the decision was reasonable. They do this by first identifying potential harm to the body that might arise from disclosing the records, and then proving that this harm is likely to happen.

> *The trade union IMPACT sought a copy of a Hazard Identification and Risk Assessment report carried out for Offaly County Council relating to County Hall building. The Council refused citing Section 20 and saying it was in draft form and that it was not in order to release it. The Information Commissioner pointed out that there is a presumption under the Act that the refusal is not justified unless the public body can prove the decision was justified. In this case, the Commissioner was critical of the decisions made by the Council and said it had made no argument that any harm would result from the release of the report. She ordered the Council to release the report.*

> *In 2008, the* **Irish Medical News** *sought a copy of a review carried out by the HSE on acute services in HSE South. The Executive refused saying the finished report was still part of ongoing consultations with staff and releasing it would cause damage to these talks thereby damaging the public interest. The Commissioner rejected that argument saying that the report was not exempt under Section 20 and ordered its release.*

As regards the public interest test, it is a matter for the deciding officer to make up their own mind whether it is in the best interests of the public to see the records. If they decide it is, then they can be released. When the body decides that the public interest is not in favour of release then an appeal should follow to the Information Commissioner. In many decisions, the Commissioner has found that the public interest is very much in favour of release.

> In 2008, Dun Laoghaire–Rathdown County Council received an FOI request seeking copies of plans and records relating to the development of Blackrock Park. The Council released some records but refused others. One document, a landscape drawing, was not mentioned by the Council at all and its existence only emerged when the applicant asked for it specifically. The Council said they had inadvertently omitted it. The Council argued that to release records they had refused would mean they would have to engage in public consultations to counter any potential misinformation created by their early release. The Commissioner pointed out that greater openness carries a burden of having to deal with increased scrutiny and as such this 'burden' could not be a reason to override the public interest in releasing information.

However, the old legal adage applies here though: what may interest the public may not necessarily be in the public interest. This means that what people may actually be interested in finding out may not serve the wider good of the public and society.

> When a request for records relating to the Review Group on Building Societies Legislation was turned down, the issue ended up with the Information Commissioner in 2004. The Department of Finance had refused to release, citing a variety of sections, including Section 20. In agreeing with the Department, the Commissioner noted that as the deliberative process relating to the building societies legislation was on-going, she did not believe that the public interest to release information of a sensitive and confidential nature about the recommendations made. She upheld the Department's decision on most records.

The deciding officer has discretion whether or not to release records and there is a public interest clause in Section 20. Either or both of these should be mentioned in an appeal and an argument made that what is being sought is in the public interest and that the decision maker should exercise discretion and release the records. It is also worth keeping an eye on the reply to see if a specific harm has been highlighted, because if it hasn't or if a relatively tenuous one has been put forward that should be examined and appealed.

Section 21

This section relates to protecting records concerning the functions and negotiations of public bodies.

o Subsection 1 – a decision maker may refuse a request if they are of the opinion that to release the records would reasonably be expected to:

- (a) prejudice the effectiveness of tests, examinations, investigations, inquiries or audits conducted by or on behalf of the body
- (b) have a significant adverse effect on the performance by an organisation of its management functions
- (c) disclose positions taken or to be taken during negotiations.

o Subsection 2 – these exemptions do not apply if the decision maker decides that public interest would best be served by releasing the records.

To claim Section 21 the decision maker must be able to show that there is a reasonable expectation that to release the records would prejudice the organisation by damaging its ability to carry out tests or inquiries. They must be able to point to specific areas where this harm would occur. They do not have to prove that the damage is probable or possible – just that their fear that it might happen is reasonable.

In previous cases, the Information Commissioner has ruled that to invoke Subsection 1(a) the organisation must show evidence of the prejudicial impact releasing the records would do. When invoking Subsection 1(b), the organisation must give an assessment of the damage that would be caused by releasing the information and prove that not only could this reasonably be expected but that the harm would be particularly damaging.

> *An FOI request for details of the salaries paid to the top twenty five presenters in RTÉ between 1998 and 2000 was rejected on the grounds that releasing such information could cause unrest between presenters and adversely affect RTÉ's management functions. The matter was appealed to the Information Commissioner. She rejected the arguments put forward by RTÉ and ordered their release. That information is now released routinely by RTÉ.*

> *In 2008 a woman who had made complaints relating to a hospital sought a copy of a report prepared by the HSE as a result. The HSE refused. On appeal the Information Commissioner ruled that the Executive had not provided any evidence that an investigation would be damaged by releasing the report and she ordered them to do so.*

And just because the organisation is conducting a review or an investigation does not mean that records cannot still be released while that is underway.

> *The* Sunday Times *newspaper sought details of payments made to a senior official, as well as mobile phone records and correspondence with a private ambulance company. Initially, the HSE said they were considering releasing the information but then decided to refuse. On appeal, the HSE said the information was part of an ongoing review and releasing the records could impact on that. The Information Commissioner criticised misleading and incomplete responses from the HSE during her investigation. Having examined the records in question, she ruled that releasing them would not harm any investigation or audit.*

While subsections (a) and (b) both require evidence of harm or damage to be done before they can prevent release, this is not the case with subsection (c). All that is required here to prevent release is that the records would disclose information or details about negotiations that are underway, will take place or have already concluded. In using this subsection, the decision maker does not need to prove or even find any examples that harm would be done. Records relating to past, present or future negotiations may be protected by this subsection. However, the definition of 'negotiation' adopted by the Commissioner is quite specific. It is 'the discussion of a matter with a view to some settlement or compromise'. If the records being sought do not come under that narrow description, then it is highly likely claiming exemption here will fail.

> *A request to the Department of Education and Science for records relating to the decision to close St. Catherine's College for Home Economics in Blackrock, County Dublin was turned down. When the matter was appealed to the Information Commissioner she rejected the Department's argument that the information was*

> *exempt from release under Section 21. The Commissioner found the Department did not specify what harm could be caused by releasing the information and so ordered the records be released.*

When using this section organisations regularly claim that to release information or records would damage trust and confidence between the organisation and its staff, contractors or other bodies. However, this has only met with limited success when considered by the Information Commissioner.

Generally, the older the document the less likely it is to impact on current negotiations or functions of the organisation. However, there is no specific time limit set down in the Act and each case has to be considered on its own merits. There is a high rate of success in appealing decisions under Section 21 at the Information Commissioner level but not always.

> *In 2005, the* Irish Times *sought records, including cost estimates, for the Government's Transport 21 plan. Some information was released but other records were not. In 2010, the Information Commissioner issued a decision in this case. She acknowledged that while time may have eroded the sensitivity of the records being sought, the Department of Transport, Iarnrod Éireann and the Railway Procurement Agency argued that even now the release of the records could impact on their ability to provide value for money in terms of contracts. The Commissioner agreed and said the information should not be released in the public interest.*

It is also important to remember that there is a public interest test in this section. This means that even if the records sought are covered by one of the earlier subsections, the deciding officer or

Commissioner can, on appeal, rule that the public interest would best be served by releasing the information.

In appealing a decision to refuse under Section 21 it is often a good idea to cite the public interest clause and back it up with a good reason as to why it is best served by releasing the information. Then find some cases where the Information Commissioner has reached a decision which would back up your argument and cite those in the appeal.

Section 22

This section covers parliamentary, legal and tribunal records.

o   Subsection 1 – orders a decision maker to refuse a request if the records being sought are:
  •   (a) exempt from production in a court because of legal professional privilege
  •   (b)if released would likely result in contempt of court
  •   (c)(i) the private papers of MEP and local councillors, (ii) if the records contain opinions, advice or recommendations or are the results of consultations considered by members of the Dáil or Seanad.

o   Subsection 1(A) – a decision maker may refuse a request if it relates to the appointment, proposed appointment, the business of, or proceedings of a tribunal set up under the Tribunal of Inquiries Act, any tribunal or body specified by the Government or a Minister which is set up to inquire into issues and has a member of the legal profession on it, or any tribunal set up by either House of the Oireachtas to inquire into issues and at the time of the request the tribunal had not finished its work.

o Subsection 1(B) – Subsection 1(A) does not apply if the record
   sought relates to the general administration of the tribunal or
   body.

o Subsection 2 – if the decision maker in the organisation is satisfied that it would be contrary to the public interest to tell the
   requester that the records they seek do or do not exist, then
   they do not have to. For example, if someone requested a copy
   of all correspondence between Mr. X and a tribunal, the tribunal could be forced to draw up a schedule of all correspondence
   with that person and then refuse to release the actual records.
   However, just by sending on a schedule it would obviously have
   confirmed that it has been in touch with Mr. X and that fact
   alone could be useful information.

The overall aim of this section is to prevent the release of private papers of politicians or legal papers (such as legal advice to a
person or organisation) and documents drawn up or received by
tribunals of inquiry.

Legal professional privilege allows a client to maintain confidential communication with their legal advisor. It is important for
the proper functioning of organisations that they can ask for and
receive legal advice in confidence. Subsection 1(b) is aimed at preventing the release of records which could cause contempt of court,
for example, if the records relate to a young child about whom
there has been an *in camera* court hearing. Subsection (1)(c) is to
ensure that most papers held by politicians are not released.

If properly applied by the organisation, then it is hard to draw
up a convincing argument that the documents should be released –
especially as there is no public interest clause in Section 22. However, that does not mean that it is always properly applied by an
organisation. The Information Commissioner has ruled on several

occasions that the body was wrong when they claimed legal professional privilege and ordered that the records should be released to
the requestor.

In 2007, Eamon Murphy lodged an FOI request with the Indus-
trial Development Authority relating to an exchange of lands in-
volving his deceased relatives and an investigation into the matter
carried out at the request of the Minister for Enterprise, Trade and
Employment. The IDA released some records but refused others on
a variety of grounds. When the matter went to the Information
Commissioner, several 'third parties' involved did not object to the
records release but the IDA and other individuals did. The IDA
said two separate legal actions were underway and claimed that
releasing the information would prejudice the course of justice
and so sought exemption under Section 22. The Commissioner dis-
agreed saying there was no evidence it would cause contempt of
court and ordered the release of the information.

Tribunals have been a major issue on the Irish political and social landscape for some time. Tribunals in themselves are not subject to the Freedom of Information Act, but often records relating
to the tribunal are held by a public body (for example, a Government Department) which is responsible for the tribunal and which
is subject to FOI. It is only possible to send in a request under the
Act to the public body responsible for the tribunal and not to the
tribunal itself.

Section 22- 1(A) gives the decision maker the power to refuse to
release records relating to an appointment to, or the actual work of,
a tribunal. However, under subsection 1(B) documents relating to
the general administration of a tribunal, for example how many

days the tribunal held hearings or how many staff it has, are not exempt and can be released.

> *In 2011 businessman Denis O'Brien submitted a Freedom of Information request to the Department of the Taoiseach about the Moriarty Tribunal and how much barristers were being paid. Having obtained the information he then released the information to the media. As well as the details of the sums involved, the request also resulted in the release of letters written between the Judge and the then Taoiseach, Brian Cowen.*

Also worth noting is that while it may seem under subsection 1(A) that the decision maker could release information about the workings or proceedings of the tribunal as the Act only states they 'may refuse' and not 'shall refuse' in Section 46 there is an explicit command that records held by a tribunal are exempt from release.

The chances of getting documents from a tribunal (other than administrative ones) while it is running are not good and an appeal to the Information Commissioner is probably unlikely to succeed. However, it maybe possible to get some records after the inquiry has concluded.

> *Following the Dunne Inquiry into the retention of children's organs the Parents for Justice Group submitted FOI requests to the National Maternity Hospital and Our Lady's Hospital for Sick Children looking for records held by the hospitals. Both refused on a variety of sections, but on appeal the Information Commissioner decided that most records held by both hospitals should be released. They were not legally privileged and there was a strong public interest in releasing them, she ruled.*

However, tribunals of inquiry established under the Commissions of Investigations Bill 2003 are largely exempt from FOI except when the record sought was created before the commission came into being or the record relates to expenses or the general administration of the commission.

Section 23

This section relates to documents surrounding law enforcement and public safety.

o   Subsection 1(a) – a decision maker may refuse a request if in their opinion it would hamper criminal investigations or prosecutions, law enforcement, lawful methods for the safety of individuals or the public, court proceedings, the safety of property or communication systems of bodies like the gardaí.

o   Subsection 1(b) – a decision maker may refuse to release records if they would reveal the identity of anyone who came forward with information in confidence.

o   Subsection 1(c) – records which would allow for an offence to take place can also be refused.

o   Subsection 2 – if the decision maker believes that to confirm or deny whether the records sought actually exist would not be in the public interest then they can refuse to release and refuse to say if the records exist.

o   Subsection 3 – none of these exclusions apply if the records sought show that the law was broken during an investigation; if the records sought relate to the performance of an organisation involved in law enforcement or public safety; or that the records relate to the success or otherwise of any programme or scheme aimed at crime prevention or solving *and* that the decision maker is of the opinion that public interest would best be served by releasing the records sought.

This Section is to ensure that public bodies which are subject to the Act do not release any documents which could damage criminal investigations or endanger public safety. The Irish Act is quite restrictive regarding law enforcement organisations. In most countries with FOI, the administrative functions of police forces are subject to FOI but not here. There is no valid reason for this exclusion – it's just more Irish secrecy. However, communications with, for example, the Department of Justice could be accessible.

The decision maker does have discretion in this area as the wording of the section says that they 'may refuse' which also equates as they 'may release' as well. This could be mentioned in an appeal, but the chances of getting information which could cause physical harm or reveal details of criminal investigations are remote – presuming that if released the records would actually result in that.

> *The Department of Justice, Equality and Law Reform received a request from the father of a victim of the Dublin/Monaghan bombings seeking some of the records held in relation to the attacks. The Department granted some but withheld others under a variety of sections. In refusing the appeal, the Commissioner pointed out that Section 23(1)(a)(iii) allows for refusals on the grounds that it would be 'reasonably expected to prejudice or impair lawful methods' for ensuring public safety and security. She said it is not designed to protect the information but rather the way the information has been gathered. She upheld the Department's decision not to release the records sought.*

The area of information given in confidence is one that resulted in several appeals to the Information Commissioner – either by people seeking to identify who passed on information or by those who gave information seeking to prevent the release of records which would identify them. These have met with varying degrees of success and the outcome very much depends on the case itself.

> *The parents against whom a complaint of child abuse had been made sought to have information released to them which would identify who contacted the health service about the allegations. The Commissioner refused their request saying the information had been given in confidence, made in good faith and it was reasonable to expect such information to remain confidential.*

> *A number of teachers in a west of Ireland school sent a letter of complaint to the Department of Education about poor working conditions. The Department acknowledged receipt in letters sent to all the teachers in the school. Those that were not involved in sending the original letter then sought a copy of it under FOI. The Commissioner ruled that the letter itself could be released to the Principal of the school but with the names of the teachers involved redacted to protect their identities.*

Subsection 3 offers several important clauses which allow for certain records to be released. Included are records which contain information regarding the efficiency of any law enforcement organisation, such as the gardaí, who are outside the remit of the Act. Also releasable are records which reveal law breaking during an investigation and records which discuss the success or failure of law enforcement policies or schemes. Obviously, this only applies if anything was committed to paper or e-mail!

For the purpose of appeals it is also worth noting that the Commissioner has adopted the approach that to claim exemption under this section, the decision maker must: (a) identify the harm which the release could cause, and (b) show that it is reasonable to expect that the harm will materialise. In an appeal to the Commissioner both criteria have to be met to her satisfaction. If either one fails then so to does the claim of exemption.

Here, too, there is also a public interest clause which would allow a decision maker to release records if they decide it is in the public interest to do so. This, as always, is worth highlighting in an appeal and pointing out how it would be in the public interest for the records to be made available.

Section 24

This section relates to information surrounding security, defence and international relations.

o   Subsection 1 – a decision maker may refuse to release records if, in their opinion, it could reasonably be expected to adversely affect:

- the security of the State, or defence of the State
- international relations of the State
- matters relating to Northern Ireland
- functions of the Commission for the Location of Victims' Remains.

o   Subsection 2 – a decision maker must refuse a request if the record sought contains: intelligence information for the security or defence of the State; operations of the Defence Forces and tackling crimes which could undermine public order or the authority of the State. However, it goes on to cover communications between the Government and a diplomatic mission or another government, information received in confidence from individuals outside the country, the European Union or other international organisation as well as records relating to negotiations with international bodies.

o   Subsection 3 – if the decision maker believes it would be contrary to the public interest to disclose whether a record sought actually exists or not, they can refuse to release and refuse to confirm whether or not the record exists.

This is something of an unusual section in that it combines two very different functions of the State together – defence and international relations – and treats them both with a fairly high degree of protection.

The first subsection allows some discretion for the decision maker as they can decide to refuse or to release records as long as they do not adversely affect the security of Ireland. Again, the onus is on the organisation to make a reasonable case on appeal that harm would occur. If the Information Commissioner decides the case is not reasonable, then the documents can be released.

> *A man who was discharged from the Defence Forces in the late 1960s, following an investigation which said he could be a security risk, made an application to the Department of Defence for all records about him. The Department refused but the Information Commissioner decided that there was nothing which could reasonably be expected to harm the interests of the State by releasing the records and ordered the Department to do so.*

Relations with other countries are also covered by this exemption, but again, the body has to prove that harm is likely before the Commissioner will accept the documents are exempt.

> *The Department of Justice refused a request from a Sunday Times journalist, Phelim McAleer, seeking copies of records relating to the Brussels II convention on the recognition of matrimonial proceedings in EU States. The Department refused but the Commissioner held that since the Department did not clearly explain how our international relations could be adversely affected, they could not successfully claim exemption under this Section. He ordered the release of most of the documents.*

The second subsection, however, removes that discretion and says requests for records which contain information relating to a wide variety of issues must be refused. Some of these are understandable, for example intelligence information or operations being conducted by the defence forces, but this section puts a blanket refusal in place for all communication with an embassy regardless of how serious or trivial the content actually is.

> *A request to the Department of Foreign Affairs seeking access to records about the Church of Scientology was refused on the grounds that it could harm our international relations. The records were reports from an Irish embassy about a foreign government's views on Scientology and actions taken by them. The Commissioner found that much of the information was already in the public domain and that releasing the records could not reasonably be expected to adversely Ireland's international relations.*

As well as diplomatic communications, information 'communicated in confidence' from every international organisation of countries can also be exempt from release under this draconian section. It is important to note that the phrase 'communicated in confidence' is not the same as 'containing confidential information'. For example, an e-mail from the World Postal Union discussing unpublished plans for new stamps could be afforded the same level of protection as a document from a security agency like the CIA about international terrorism.

Unsurprisingly, there is no public interest clause here but there are those all important word at the start of the Section – 'may refuse' – which also means the decision maker may also decide to release. It is worth highlighting that in an appeal to the Commissioner.

It may also be worth arguing that the records being sought are not actually capable of being exempted under this Section and therefore they should be released.

Section 25

This Section deals with the issuing of Ministerial Certificates.

o   Subsection 1 – a Minister may issue a certificate which prevents the release of documents referred to in Sections 23 and 24 (law enforcement and public safety; security defence and international relations).

This section is unusual in that it is entirely devoted to how records can be prevented from release. A Minister can only issue certificates if they are satisfied that the records are of sufficient sensitivity or seriousness to justify their actions, and they can only do so after the head of the body requests them to.

These certificates must be reviewed every two years, but not by the Minister who issued the certificate. The review is carried out instead by other members of the Government who are, in reality, unlikely to go against the views of a Cabinet colleague. There is no appeal to the Information Commissioner once a certificate has been issued and the only option is to take a High Court action.

Like the other subsections which grant powers to issue certificates, this is a very powerful tool for the State as it effectively halts the release of some records which probably should be made public. No reason has to be given by the Minister for their decision to issue a certificate. All the Act says is that they have to be 'satisfied that the record is of sufficient sensitivity or seriousness to justify his or her doing so'.

In choosing to cite this section, the Department and Minister are effectively shutting the door on the public and ensuring the Information Commissioner has no involvement. There are many other sections which could be used in good faith to prevent the release of records which could cause genuine harm. However, by choosing those sections the decision maker could be subject to review by the Commissioner. This section removes that option. The only route of appeal from here is to the High Court, which would be both costly and time consuming.

A ministerial certificate lasts two years but can be extended and renewed every two years without limit.

Section 26

This section relates to the protection of information obtained in confidence and those who provided it.

o   Subsection 1 – a decision maker shall refuse a request if the record contains:

- information given in confidence to a public body on the understanding it would be treated as confidential and if, in the opinion of the decision maker, disclosure would jeopardise the future flow of information
  - if a decision to release would result in a breach of a duty of confidence provided for in an agreement or by law.

o Subsection 2 – the exemption does not apply to a record created by a member of staff of the organisation or someone providing a service to the organisation unless disclosure would result in a breach of duty or confidence included in an agreement or in law.

o Subsection 3 – if, in the opinion of the decision maker, the public interest would best be served by releasing information given in confidence then they may do so. This applies to subsection 1(a) only though.

o Subsection 4 – if a decision maker is of the opinion that to disclose whether they have the records or not would jeopardise the future flow of information from the source, then they can refuse to say whether the documents being sought actually exist.

The many organisations of the State receive information in confidence all the time, and this section is aimed at protecting the information and those that provide it from exposure once certain criteria are met.

To get an exemption from release under this section, the organisation has to be able to prove that the information was not only given in confidence but that releasing it would also possibly stop similar information being given in the future. If releasing the information could result in a legal breach of confidence then an FOI request can also be turned down.

> When the then Department of Social, Family and Community Affairs received an anonymous letter alleging a man was working while claiming benefit it was investigated and found to be untrue. The man sought a copy of the letter under FOI but the Department refused. The Commissioner agreed with that decision, saying the handwriting could reveal the identity of the person, that it was important the Department continue to receive confidential information and that the public interest was in maintaining that and not releasing the letter.

However subsection (2) states clearly that if the records being sought were written by a member of staff or by an outside contractor on behalf of the organisation, then they cannot be exempted on confidentiality grounds except in cases where releasing the documents would create a breach of duty or confidence.

If a decision maker decides to release information under this section, then they have to contact the person or persons who supplied it. That person also has the right to appeal to the Information Commissioner to prevent records being released if, in their view, it could lead to them being identified or cause a breach of trust. Under Section 29, the organisation has two weeks from the receipt of the FOI request to contact the person, company or body who supplied the information. They then have three weeks (plus another two weeks if the case is complex) to make submissions to the decision maker arguing, presumably, why the information should not be released. The deciding officer will then determine whether or not the records should be released.

When the Department of Agriculture and Food decided to release information about two poultry processing companies they were contacted and told of the decision. They appealed that decision to the Information Commissioner arguing it was a breach of confidentiality. The Commissioner rejected their arguments saying there was significant public interest in hygiene and food safety control in meat processing operations.

There are several points worth making in appealing a decision not to release under this section. Firstly, there is a public interest clause which covers Subsection 1(a) but not Subsection 1(b). Here it is possible to argue, if the information relates to yourself, that it is important you have the ability to see any unfounded or unfair allegations that may have been made against you. While malicious allegations known to have been false will not be protected under this subsection, the Commissioner has ruled on several occasions that wrong information given when genuinely believed, can be exempt from release under Section 26, including the identity of the person or organisation who provided the information.

There are four separate elements to Subsection 1(a), all of which must be met before the exemption can be relied on: (a) the information was given in confidence; (b) it was given on the understanding it would be treated as confidential; (c) its disclosure would be likely to prejudice similar information being given by the person; and (d) it is so important to the organisation that it must continue to be able to receive it in confidence.

In relation to Subsection 1(b) the Information Commissioner's office has ruled that there are three elements that have to be satisfied before this can be properly invoked. The information must: (a) have the necessary quality of confidence about it; (b) have been given in circumstances where there is an obligation of confidence;

and (c) that unauthorised use of the information would be harmful to the person or body who communicated it. If the Commissioner finds that any of the criteria have not been met, then the exemption does not apply and the records should be released.

It is also important to note that if the information came from a member of staff of the organisation arising from their work, it could be claimed that Subsection 2 should result in disclosure.

There have been several cases where a Department claimed that the flow of information to it would cease if records were to be released, but when the Information Commissioner's office contacted the organisation supplying the information they actually had no objection to it being released at all. Just because someone says releasing information would cause harm does not actually mean it will. And just because a record has 'strictly private and confidential' written on it does not make it exempt from release either. The Commissioner's view is that the contents of the record are the deciding factor.

The Department of Enterprise, Trade and Employment refused to give a work permit to Daniel Reed to work as Technical Director of Coaching and Marketing Director of the Dublin Lightning American football team. Although this was later reversed, Mr. Reed sought access to records on which the Department had made its original decision. It emerged there were differences between two different groups within the American football fraternity in Ireland and information was provided by one group 'in confidence' about Mr. Reed. The Commissioner decided that the information should be released on the grounds that releasing it could not jeopardise the future flow of information and the public interest outweighed claims of confidentiality.

In another case, the Commissioner held that where people have professional responsibilities to pass information to another person or organisation, such as gardaí or health care professionals, then this section cannot be cited to prevent records being released. The idea is that they are bound to pass on the information regardless of whether the records are released or not. Overall, this section is aimed at protecting 'whistleblowers' who are not bound to pass on information and could suffer if their identity became known.

Appeals by people who supplied information to a public body in the belief it was in confidence only to be informed that the organisation is considering releasing it on foot of an FOI request have to convince the Commissioner that the information was of importance and that releasing it would cause harm to them in some form.

Those asked to supply character references for people seeking jobs or promotions should also be aware that the Commissioner has found that such references cannot be exempt from the Act regardless of the content or whether those providing the information were assured it would be treated as confidential. It will not be!

When the Sunday Times *newspaper sought details of an out of court settlement between the then North Eastern Health Board and a medical consultant, it was refused on various grounds including the fact there was a confidentiality clause in the agreement which prevented the release of any information.*

Although the Commissioner stressed that each case would be treated separately, she overturned a decision to refuse and said that organisations with responsibility for spending public money could not automatically assume that such confidentiality agreements would be exempt from release under the Act.

Commercially, certain parts of a tendering process can be exempt under this Section too, but the Commissioner has found that when an agreement has been reached this section may no longer apply in areas such as pricing etc. The Commissioner has applied strict criteria before this exemption can be invoked, and most appeals seeking the records are granted.

There is no public interest clause here so the arguments in an appeal must centre on the validity of citing this section to prevent the release of information. Depending on the request, it could be argued that public spending should be open to close public scrutiny or that there is an over-riding personal reason why the records being sought should be released.

Section 27

This section is aimed at protecting commercially sensitive information from being released under the Act.

- o Subsection 1 – a decision maker shall refuse to release the records if they contain:
  - trade secrets of someone other than the person making the FOI request
  - sensitive information which could reasonably be expected to result in a loss or gain to the person or business to whom the information applies
  - information which could prejudice the outcome of contractual or other negotiations.

- o Subsection 2 – the decision maker shall grant the request if
  - the person to whom the record relates consents
  - similar information is available to the public
  - the records relate to the requester

- if the person who supplied the information was informed before it was given that it might be made available to the public
- disclosure is necessary to avoid a serious and imminent danger to life or health or the environment.

o Subsection 3 – if the decision maker is of the opinion that the public interest is best served by releasing the information then it can be released.

o Subsection 4 – if the decision maker believes that if by acknowledging whether records exist or not it could cause problems then they shall refuse the request and not disclose whether the records do exist or not.

Obviously various State organisations will receive commercially sensitive information every day. It could range from economic plans, concerns about a particular large employer or tender documents, for example. There are good reasons why much of this type of information is exempt as release could harm the State or the company which provided the information, such as details of commercial transactions.

However, the Commissioner has found on several occasions that the public interest in this section is best served by releasing details. For example, this could include successful and unsuccessful tenders that are to some degree at least 'historical', that is, are not part of a current competition. To claim exemption under Section 27, the State body or the commercial company has to be able to show that the records either contain trade secrets or that harm could 'reasonably' be expected to occur if the information was released.

However, it must be remembered that simply stating harm will arise is not sufficient, and while that may work in an internal appeal it almost certainly will not with an appeal to the Commissioner. That office will ask for evidence that harm is possible. And even if the Commissioner's office accepts that there could be some commercial value to the records, the public interest then has to be considered and that could result in the records being released.

> *One of the most important decisions regarding commercially sensitive information came in a case where a request was received by the Department of Defence from Mark Henry of Policywatch seeking details of a contract to supply army vehicles. The Office of Public Works agreed to release the information but three of the four companies who successfully tendered for the contract, Ford, Nissan and Motor Distributors, all objected to the release. MAN Importers Ireland Ltd. also objected but did not do so formally. The companies argued that their tender bids contained commercially sensitive information and that release could damage their competitive position. However, the Information Commissioner ruled that the tender price could not be a trade secret after the competition had closed and although he accepted there could be commercial harm caused, he decided that the public interest outweighed that and he dismissed the appeal.*

This has been followed through on several occasions where the Commissioner's office has found that although there is a commercial sensitivity surrounding the records sought, the public interest was stronger and the records should be released.

However, this is by no means guaranteed, and the Commissioner's office is well aware of sensitivities surrounding commercial transactions.

> *A request seeking a list of companies likely to make staff re-dundant was turned down by the then Department of Enterprise, Trade and Employment. On appeal, the Information Commissioner decided that even being known to be on such a list would disclose sensitive commercial information and would not be in the public interest. The Department's decision was upheld.*

As with the previous section, if the State organisation is considering releasing records relating to a third party, that person or company must be informed of the possible release and then given a chance to appeal to the Information Commissioner before it happens. On occasion the Commissioner has found in favour of withholding information in these third party appeals, but such decisions are rare.

Appeals seeking the release of information should set out reasonable grounds as to why it is in the public interest to make records available. It is also worthwhile mentioning that if spending of public money is involved, it is important that such spending is open for all to see. The argument could also be made that the records do not fall under the remit of this section and that the decision to cite it was wrong so the records should be released.

Section 28

This section relates to information regarding individuals and held by a State body.

o   Subsection 1 – a decision maker shall refuse a request if, in their opinion, it would disclose personal information, including information about someone who is dead.

o   Subsection 2 – information can be released if:
    •   it relates to the requestor

- the person to whom the information relates consents to its release
- similar information is generally available to the public
- the person supplied information about themselves and was informed that it might be made available to the public
- disclosure is necessary to avoid imminent danger to the life or health of an individual.

o Subsection 3 – if the records relate to sensitive medical information about the requester, the decision maker can refuse to release if they believe disclosure would be prejudicial to the requester's physical or mental health, well-being or emotional condition.

o Subsection 4(a) – if this is the case the records can instead be released to a medical professional.

o Subsection 5(a) – if the decision maker believes the public interest outweighs the right to privacy of the individual, they can release the records.

o Subsection 5(b) – if the decision maker believes it would be to the benefit of the person involved, then the records can be released.

o Subsection 5(A) – if the decision maker believes disclosure of whether records being sought actually exist could cause harm, then they can refuse to state whether the documents do exist or not.

o Subsection 5(B) – if an individual seeks records about themselves but in releasing that information it would disclose details of other individuals, then the decision maker shall refuse to release the records.

This section is designed to protect personal information by preventing its release to other people under the Act. There is a public interest clause in this section (subsection 5(a)) that can be cited if appealing a decision to refuse or limit access to records.

In particular cases where a person seeks records about themselves, the State (usually the HSE) can cite subsection 3 if they believe it is not in the person's best interest, or they can release the records instead to a medical professional who can then talk to the requestor in person about the records. In many cases the Commissioner has rejected appeals relating to this area.

> *In 2008 a man sought copies of medical records held by the HSE about him but was refused on the basis that it could have a negative impact on him. During the appeal, the Information Commissioner offered to release the information to a doctor but the man refused. His appeal was turned down.*

This is the section that has been frequently relied upon in health and welfare cases where an individual seeks access to records about themselves or their family. The Commissioner has been reluctant to intrude too far in releasing personal information in such cases by upholding decisions to refuse or limit release. However, when medical concerns are not an issue the approach has generally been that people are entitled to see records that relate to them with the identity of other individuals removed from the document.

An individual's remuneration is very definitely personal information but there has been a growing but slow acceptance that when the tax payer is paying there is a strong public interest in disclosing this information.

> *In 1999, Richard Oakley of the* Sunday Tribune *sought details of expenses paid to Oireachtas members. This was opposed by most of the political parties. However, the Information Commissioner ruled that the public interest in how money was spent outweighed the right to privacy of the Oireachtas members.*

Since that ruling, details of expenses paid to our TDs and Senators are released by the Houses of the Oireachtas. There was also a very significant decision by the Department of Finance in 2010 relating to the pay of senior public sector workers.

> *Michael Somers was a Chief Executive of the National Treasury Management Agency and objected when the Department of Finance told him they were going to release details of his pay following an FOI request. In her ruling the Commissioner said the appeal by the former CEO to stop the release must fail because he had not met the burden of proof that it was not in the public interest to know how much he was paid.*

And it's not just individuals. The Commissioner's office has frequently made rulings in favour of releasing information about State payments. In a 2001 judgement, the Commissioner stated that the release of information about significant business transactions by public bodies 'should be the norm unless it would involve the disclosure of personal information and the consequential intrusion on the privacy of the recipients would outweigh the benefits of openness and transparency'.

However, seeking access to records relating to an individual's work is unlikely to succeed. The Commissioner has found in decisions that those who work in bodies subject to the Act are entitled to privacy about their personal records, work evaluations and competence. As a result, there would have to be strong public interest grounds evident before the Commissioner would be likely to reverse this trend and release such records.

In making appeals against this section, always cite why the public interest would be served by releasing the information. Also, it is worth arguing that the public is entitled to see what is being done with public money and who is receiving it. Again, back up any argument – if possible – with previous decisions which support it.

Section 30

This section is aimed at protecting research as well as the country's natural resources.

o Subsection 1 – a decision maker may refuse to release records if, in their opinion, it:

- contains information on research being done or to be done by or on behalf of a public organisation and its disclosure or its disclosure before the research has concluded would expose the organisation, an individual or the subject of the research to serious disadvantage
- could reasonably be expected to prejudice the well being of a cultural, heritage or natural resource of a species the habitat of a species or flora or fauna.

o Subsection 2 – if the decision maker decides it would be in the public interest to release the records sought, then they can be released.

This is another odd collection of issues protected under one section of the Act. Research on any topic and the protection of flora and fauna are not normally linked.

Subsection 1 allows for research being undertaken or to be done on behalf of a public body to be exempt from release. This could range from financial, social, health or in fact anything that could be classed as research. However it cannot be claimed that the research records cannot be released simply because they are part of a research project. To claim the exemption, the body would have to prove that its disclosure would expose someone or some organisation to serious disadvantage.

Subsection 2 says that if releasing documents could, for example, identify the location of a rare species that would be at risk, then the deciding officer can refuse to release. This would also apply to historic buildings or archaeological sites.

> *The then Department of Arts, Heritage, Gaeltacht and the Islands received a request for records detailing the location of the special areas of conservation for the protection of a fresh water mussel. It refused to release that information on the grounds that it could reasonably be expected to prejudice the well-being of the species. The Commissioner found that the public interest was best served by withholding the information and rejected the appeal.*

Although it didn't succeed in that case, there are two elements which could be argued when trying to secure release of records where a decision to refuse or limit has been made citing this section. The first is that the decision maker has discretion under subsection 1 and that should favour release. The second is that subsection 2 has a public interest clause and that too should favour release.

Section 31

This section was created to protect the financial and economic interests of the State and public bodies.

o Subsection 1 – a decision maker may refuse a request if, in their opinion:

- access to the record could reasonably be expected to have a serious adverse affect on the financial interests of the State or on the ability of the Government to manage the national economy
- premature disclosure of the information could reasonably be expected to result in undue disturbance of the ordinary course of business generally, or in any specific area
- access to the record could reasonably be expected to result in unfair benefit or loss to someone or people generally.

o Subsection 2 says it applies to records relating to:

- rates of currency exchange
- taxes or other forms of revenue
- interest rates
- borrowings
- regulation or supervision by or on behalf of the State by a public body of banking, insurance or other financial business
- securities or foreign currency trading
- regulation or control by or on behalf of the State or a public body of wages, salaries or prices
- proposals relating to State spending
- property transactions or proposed transactions involving property
- foreign investment in the State
- industrial development in the State
- international trade
- trade, financial, commercial, industrial scientific and or technical secrets which belong to the State or a public body and is of substantial value or likely to be of substantial value

- all information which could reasonably be expected to adversely affect the competitive position of a public body in relation to its commercial activities
- the economic or financial circumstances of a public body.

o Subsection 3 – the exclusions do not apply if, in the opinion of the head, the public interest would best be served by granting the request.

Given the crisis that enveloped the country, this section is probably one of the most important in the Act. As noted before, the State has traditionally been adverse to the idea of openness and many of the key financial organisations, such as the National Treasury Management Agency and the Central Bank, have all been deliberately kept outside of FOI. This decision sends a clear signal that what these vital bodies do with vast amounts of public money is not something the public should know about in detail. The only information available is what these organisations or the Government choose to put out into the public domain.

The Commission has highlighted on several occasions the fact that such important public bodies are still outside the remit of FOI. Emily O'Reilly has repeatedly argued that they should not be and that there is plenty of scope within this section to protect sensitive information. All to no avail, as these organisations remain outside the scope of FOI. The Department of Finance, on the other hand, is subject to the Act.

Protecting the financial interests of the State is of huge importance and there are plenty of restrictions available under this section of the Act which do just that. Subsection 1 states that the deciding officer just has to form the opinion that disclosure of the records 'could reasonably be expected' to have serious consequences. They do not have to prove it or even that it is likely – just that it could be expected to cause harm and that the expectation is reasonable.

Subsection 2 lists the type of records that are covered. It is an extensive list but records not listed here may or may not be exempt from release under the Act too. There is only one way to find out and that is to request them.

In an appeal it could be pointed out that the appeal officer is allowed a choice whether to release and that there is also a public interest clause. A convincing argument would have to be drawn up to prove that the records being sought are in the public interest and that harm, if any, is outweighed by this interest.

A body cannot claim that just because the record relates to a particular topic it is automatically exempt. The organisation has to point to specific parts of a record or records and argue that release would be likely to have a 'serious adverse affect'. The threshold is pretty low, however, as and noted earlier the organisation only has to prove that it is reasonable to expect this harm.

Section 32

This section is designed as a secrecy catch-all.

- o Subsection 1 – a decision maker shall refuse a request if:
  - disclosure of the record is prohibited by any other law
  - any law authorises a decision maker not to release the record.

- o Subsection 2 – a joint committee of the Oireachtas can:
  - review any law that authorises or allows for records to be withheld having regard to the purpose and spirit of this Act
  - publish the review.

o   Subsection 3 – a Government minister may publish a report with or without recommendations regarding changing secrecy provisions in other laws to allow records be released under this Act.

This section is designed to be a 'catch-all' and says that decision makers must refuse to release records if their release is against any other law.

> *In 2003 the Commissioner upheld a decision by the Department of Justice, Equality and Law Reform to refuse to release records (if they existed) about alleged phone tapping of the requestor's home. The Commissioner agreed that the Interceptions of Postal Packets and Telecommunications Messages (Regulations) Act 1993 outlawed the confirmation of such records, and therefore the documents, if they existed, cannot be released.*

And it is not just matters of national security that are protected under this section. The range of records is quite large and covers everything from secret intelligence files to school reports.

> *When a request was made to access the results attained in the Junior and Leaving Certificate exams in all schools for 1998 and 1999, the Department of Education refused on the grounds that Section 53 of the Education Act 1998 allows the Department to refuse to release information which would allow someone to compare results from different schools. The Commissioner upheld the decision to refuse to release.*

In comparison, such information about schools in the UK is routinely released. There is no public interest clause with this section and refusal is mandatory if the deciding officer rules that the records fall under subsection (a) or (b). An appeal to the Commissioner is only likely to succeed on the basis that the exemption was incorrectly applied and that the records do not fall under either category.

Section 46

This Section outlines further restrictions to the Act that are not mentioned earlier. In fact it lists a wide range of areas which are not subject to the Act

o   Subsection 1 – the Act does not apply to:
    - a record held by the courts or tribunals
    - records held or created by the Attorney General or the office, the Director of Public Prosecutions or the office
    - investigations carried out by the Comptroller and Auditor General and the Ombudsman
    - records relating to the President
    - (d)(a) any costing of proposals done for any political party
    - (d)(b) any record given by a public body to a Minister or Minister of State for their use in any debate in the Oireachtas
    - (e) private papers of any member of the Oireachtas
    - (f) any record which could identify anyone who gave information in confidence relating to the enforcement of criminal law.

o   However, these exemptions do not apply to:
    - (a)(I) records not created by courts or tribunals, but which relate to their proceedings in public and whose disclosure is not forbidden
    - (a)(II) records which relate the general administration of courts or tribunals, Director of Public Prosecutions and Attorney General

- (c)(I) records created before a review, investigation or audit carried out by the Ombudsman or Comptroller and Auditor General gets underway
- (c)(II) records which relate to the general administration of the office of the Comptroller and Auditor General or office of the Ombudsman.

o Subsection 2 – the Act does not apply to:
- records that are available for public inspection either free or for a fee
- records which are available to purchase.

Subsection 1 outlines the various parts of the State apparatus which are exempt from FOI, many for understandable reasons. Tribunals, courts and the State prosecution agencies should be able to do their work without fear of records being released under the Act. It's a similar case for members of the Oireachtas in that they could receive a lot of personal information or create documents which, if available for public scrutiny, could limit or hinder their work.

Since the Comptroller and Auditor General as well as the Ombudsman's offices would receive records while carrying out examinations it is easy to see why they are exempt in that it is necessary to prevent the release records during or after that review.

The same cannot be said, however, for every record relating to the President, which as a result of this section is automatically exempt regardless of their content. There is no valid reason for this exemption to exist. There are many other sections which prevent the release of information but this blanket ban only serves to limit the scope of the public's ability to find out what is being done on their behalf.

Why every paper given to a Minister to brief them for an Oireachtas debate should be exempt also serves no benefit except to keep information withheld. If a Minister is not asked the right question, they do not have to give all the information they have at their disposal. And with this exemption, the information cannot be readily found out afterwards either by FOI.

There has been an increasing move towards openness in this area with several departments putting briefing documents for newly appointed Ministers on their website. However, regular briefing documents are not put up. The issue again is that the Department can choose what they want the public to see.

Functions of organisations which were subject to FOI have been removed from the remit of public scrutiny including, for example, records held by the Health and Safety Authority arising from its enforcement functions.

> *Following a workplace accident, the HSA received an FOI request seeking guidelines and advice issued to an employer subsequent to the incident. The Authority refused saying that Section 74 of the Safety, Health and Welfare at Work Act, 2005 meant that such records were outside the reach of FOI. The Commissioner agreed and refused an appeal seeking release of the information.*

It is clear that this section is very different from all the other sections in the Act. Where they say a deciding officer shall refuse or may refuse, this section is very clear in that the Act simply does not apply to those records. There is no public interest clause. Once the organisation is satisfied that the record relates to one of the various elements mentioned then that's it – the document is exempt. The only possibility of appeal to the Information Commissioner lies on the argument that the records do not relate to one of the eight specific areas listed in subsection 1. It is also worth mentioning that just because a record can be refused under FOI, the public body can still choose to release it if it so desires.

Subsection 1 does allow access to, for example, records which relate to the administration of tribunals, courts, the DPP or AG's office, the C&AG and Ombudsman's office, for example. This could relate to staffing issues, rates of pay for counsel, number of days people worked and so on.

But what about records held by a public body as well as, for example, the gardai or the Director of Public Prosecutions? In an interesting ruling, the Commissioner decided that these are not outside the ambit of FOI.

When records from the Environmental Protection Agency about an investigation into a company where copies of records were sent to the DPP, the EPA refused citing a number of sections including 46. The Agency argued with the Information Commissioner that it would circumvent the protection granted to the DPP if records could be accessed via a body which is subject to the Act. The Commissioner, however, didn't agree and said they were subject to the Act and should be released.

Subsection 2 makes clear that if the records are available for inspection by members of the public, for example planning files, then they are exempt from release under the Act. If someone wants these records they can either go and view them or buy a copy.

Appeals under Section 46 are tricky to say the least. The best argument is probably that the section is being cited incorrectly and that the records should be released. However, it would be a good idea to be able to back up that argument with other similar examples.

6

Access to Information on the Environment (AIE)

WHILE THE **FREEDOM OF INFORMATION ACT** is better known and used far more frequently, an EU Directive called Access Information on the Environment (AIE) is also an extremely valuable tool for those seeking information about the activities of the State. It is both more limiting and more expansive than FOI – limiting in that the information that can be sought is more restrictive, but more expansive in that it covers all public bodies.

This particular piece of legislation is designed to give widespread access to information about the environment, and to encourage much wider public participation and understanding about the State's actions in relation to the environment. Even the word 'environment' has a very broad definition under the Directive to maximise its reach. However, when transposing the Directive into Irish law, the then Government brought in limits and fees which are unique to this country.

So far, there's been very little use here of Access to Information on the Environment legislation but that will change over time as more people become aware of it. However, it probably will always play second fiddle to FOI.

The Access to Information on the Environment legislation came into force on May 1, 2007 as a result of EU directive 2003/4/EU, replacing an earlier Directive. While FOI laws vary around the EU, the Directive is generally the same. Citizens of one country can also apply to another jurisdiction to access records under AIE. And there is also one other significant issue - submitting AIE requests in Ireland, as is in all other EU countries, is free (FOI is not) although charges may be imposed for photocopying and other similar activities. Although there is no amount specified in the Directive, it does state that the charges should be reasonable, that is, they should not be used as a deterrent to people making applications.

As such, it is interesting to note that when introducing the Directive into Irish law, the Government took the opportunity to insert a clause which means that an appeal to the Environmental Commissioner here costs €150.00, the same as an appeal to the Information Commissioner. However, there is no mention of such a fee in the original EU legislation, and most other countries have not sought to impose an appeal fee.

As noted, the aim of the Directive is to encourage more public awareness of the environment and participation in the issues involved by making State information as available as possible. The hope is that the effective participation of the public would contribute to better decision making on environmental matters and eventually lead to a better environment. The law was introduced across Europe to provide an equal platform so that all citizens could use the same legislation regardless of their government's enthusiasm for such openness.

The Directive is a relatively straightforward piece of legislation. It was originally passed by the European Union in 2003 but it took another four years before it was transposed into Irish legislation. Environmental information is defined in very, very broad terms and covers information in written, visual, electronic, aural or other material form – just like FOI.

Section 3 is the heart of the Directive. It outlines in reasonable detail the scope of information covered by AIE, such as the state of air, water and landscape; factors such as radiation or waste likely to affect the environment; policies, legislation or plans likely to affect the environment; reports on the implementation of environmental legislation; and the final section which covers 'the state of human health and safety', including, for example contamination of food, built structures (such as houses) inasmuch as they could be affected by the environment.

Section 3 also goes on to detail what type of body is covered by AIE and this is where it gets really interesting. Under FOI the organisation has to be specifically mentioned to be covered by the Act, but not so under AIE. The Directive covers all public authorities and those acting on behalf of a public authority. Naturally, this includes all Government Departments and any individual performing or responsible for public administrative functions – sounds very like the Freedom of Information Act so far.

But now it starts to widen its scope. Any State body or board established by law is subject to AIE, as is any company in which all the shares are either held directly by a Government Minister, by directors appointed by a Minister or by a company which has public administrative functions and responsibilities. This would include, for example, all semi-state companies such as Bord na Mona or Bus Éireann which are outside the remit of the Freedom of Information Act. However, the Directive does not cover 'public authorities' acting in a judicial or legislative capacity, such as the courts.

Making an application under AIE is similar to FOI, and so too is the process the public body undertakes to reach a decision on whether to release information or not. However, the Irish implementation of the Directive differs significantly from the original on the issue of refusals, and unsurprisingly, the aim here is to limit its scope and power. The EU version only says that Member States 'may' refuse a request in certain conditions, while the Irish version says some requests must be refused. By doing this, in effect the Irish Government added several conditions outside the scope of the original Directive to prevent the release of information which is available for release in most other EU countries.

Another significant limitation imposed in Ireland is the exclusion of records relating to the proceedings of public authorities where such confidentially is protected by law here. The Irish Regulations specifically mentions the restrictive Freedom of Information Act, and says that records exempt under that Act are also exempt under this Directive.

The guidelines prepared by what was then the Department of the Environment, Heritage and Local Government for local authorities to use when considering AIE requests are quite blunt on just how restrictive decision makers must be. If the records being sought relate to the proceedings of public bodies, then the decision maker should take into account the far more restrictive Freedom of Information Act. The guidelines state that if the records were 'capable of being protected under FOI', then a public authority 'must not release this information under these Regulations'.

This is a very far reaching statement in that by using the word 'capable' decision makers are being told that because some element of a separate piece of legislation says they do not have to release, even if they want and believe a record should be made available, they can't do so! Again, it is no surprise that the EU original Directive contains no such order.

The guidelines specifically highlight the 'very considerable level of protection available under FOI' to meetings of the Government (thanks to the much expanded definition of what the Government is in the 2003 amendment that covers a lot!) and goes on to state that 'this level of protection should be applied, in full, to relevant requests under the AIE regulations'.

The guidelines also state that environmental information relating to anything that is or was the subject of any legal proceedings or formal inquiry – including proceedings instituted by the European Commission against Ireland – may be refused. Ireland has been the subject of several actions by the Commission and the State's interpretation of the Directive means that all these could well be exempt from release.

So the inference is clear – when it comes to issues where decision makers have discretion whether to release or refuse, once again the emphasis seems to be very much on refusing.

Public authorities are 'not obliged to make available material that is incomplete or in preliminary or other draft form' according to the Irish interpretation, and the guidelines go on to state this might apply, in particular, to reports or studies.

On the bright side, the guidelines are just that – guidelines! They are not legally binding, and that is an issue that would have to be pursued if records are refused based on the Irish guidelines rather than the actual wording of the Directive.

The guidelines do say that when considering a request, the public body should start from a position of presuming that the information should be released. However, given the multiple opportunities presented in the Irish interpretation, if a public body wanted to refuse to release records, they could find ample scope to do so.

Regarding internal communications, the guidelines highlight the fact that these too can be exempt from release, but it points out that this exemption is discretionary and warns that invoking this clause should not be resorted to 'as a simple expedient to protect all internal communications in circumstances where it would be unreasonable to do so'. Public authorities should not use this protection unless there are 'good and substantial' reasons to do so.

The Regulations state early on that records relating to emissions into the environment should be released in almost all circumstances. The Irish guidelines warn decision makers that this is a 'very significant provision that limits the powers of public authorities to refuse to disclose environmental information'. However, it then goes on to say that this should be interpreted as actual emissions, and does not include information on plans for emissions which have yet to occur.

Either way, discussions of emissions at a Government meeting remain outside the remit of the Regulations, according to the guidelines. The issue of Cabinet confidentiality is repeatedly mentioned in these guidelines and it is 'strongly suggested' to a public body that the 'public interest' clauses in the Regulations should always uphold the principle of Cabinet confidentiality regardless of the circumstances.

Although access laws like AIE have existed in one form or another since the early 1990s, they have been remarkably underutilised. The main reason for this is lack of awareness by the public and the media, coupled with an unwillingness by the State to address this information deficit and promote the existence of the regulation.

A cynical but probably accurate view is that to highlight the existence of AIE would only mean more work for the public authorities involved and pesky people accessing information the organisation would rather they did not get.

The Commissioner for Environmental Information, the person to whom appeals are made, is also the Information Commissioner, Emily O'Reilly. Legally, however, these are two separate offices.

In a speech in 2008, Ms. O'Reilly commented that it is:

'. . . an indisputable fact that AIE has not, and is not, making any significant impact in terms of making environmental information available to the public. This, I feel, is
a great pity and something we should be concerned
about.'

In the intervening years nothing has changed to alter that view.

Given the importance of the environment and 'green' issues
over the last number of years, it is surprising that AIE is still so unknown and therefore so unused. In fact, only 270 applications made
between May 1, 2007 and December 31, 2008 were accepted by Government Departments out of 323 made. A total of 217 were answered in part or in full, while 53 were rejected completely. In comparison, there were 12,672 FOI applications in 2008 alone and
mostly to the same bodies. It is indisputable that AIE is little
known and not much has been done to rectify that.

The figures from the 2010 annual report show little improve-
ment. There were 23 appeals to the Commissioner during the year
as compared to 220 appeals under the Freedom of Information Act.
Half of the AIE appeals related to Government departments, while
other bodies such as CIE, Coillte, the Commissioner for Energy
Regulation, Eirgrid and UCD made up the remainder. The fee of
€150.00 is undoubtedly a factor in so few appeals being made to her
office.

In 2008, the first full year of the new regulations, there were just
12 appeals to the Commissioner and since then the numbers have
not increased dramatically. In 2009, the number of appeals rose to
18 from 12 individuals while the 2010 figures of 23 appeals also come
from just 12 individuals. So it is clear that there is a long way before
the regulations catch on as much as the Freedom of Information
Act.

Directive 2003/4/EC, to give it its full title, came as a result of
the 1998 Aarhus Convention which was negotiated among the

countries of the United Nations Economic Commission for Europe. The then Secretary General of the UN, Kofi Annan, described it as 'the most ambitious venture in environment democracy undertaken under the auspices of the United Nations'.

The Aarhus Convention has three separate elements which are its core – the right to know, the right to participate and the right to access justice in relation to the environment. The purpose of allowing access to such information is to ensure that 'members of the public can understand what is happening in the environment around them. It also ensures that the public is able to participate in an informed manner', according to the Aarhus Convention Implementation Guide, which was published by the United Nations Economic Commission for Europe.

In its overall scope there are several similarities between the Freedom of Information Act and the Access to Information on the Environment regulations. Making a request is similar as is the appeals process. But there are some important differences too.

The differences are that while FOI is restricted to certain State bodies you can request almost anything from them. AIE, on the other hand, covers a much larger range of bodies and has fewer exemptions than FOI, but the scope of what can be requested is more limited. It is, of course, possible to use FOI to get information on the environment but there are three issues with this: (1) that it will cost €15.00 to make the application (and €75.00 for an internal appeal) while AIE is free at the application and initial appeal stages; (2) FOI offers the organisation more opportunities to refuse a request than AIE; and (3) far more organisations are covered by AIE than FOI.

The aim of the legislation is simple – to make it easier for the citizens of the European Union to find out environmental information from their government, local or national, in a simple, straight forward fashion. It acknowledges that differences among the laws in different countries relating to accessing environmental information can create inequality. Unfortunately, Ireland's approach to transposing this Directive into law has been limited and short-sighted. It certainly is in breach of the spirit of the Directive as it varies considerably in parts from the EU original.

In one example, there is no mention of fees for appeals anywhere in the Directive – except for Ireland where the then FF/PD government insisted on their imposition when drafting the regulation that would give effect to the Directive. That approach of demanding a €150.00 fee to appeal to the Commissioner for Environmental Information was decided by the Government because, as the then Minister for the Environment Dick Roche stated, it would be 'desirable and consistent with the position that pertains under FOI'.

However, the Commissioner, Emily O'Reilly, has described this fee as 'excessive' and a 'deterrent to applicants' who seek to appeal decisions. It is, she wrote in a letter to the Department of the Environment, 'particularly difficult to defend in cases of 'non-reply'. This is were a public authority doesn't reply to a request and internal appeal within the time limit which means the requestor has no option but to fork out €150.00 to try to get an answer.

And this is just one of several examples of how Ireland's approach has been dramatically less open than the original Directive. The European version states that:

o There should be a list of public authorities available – that has not been done here

o Information officers who people can contact to get environmental information should be designated – that has largely not been done

o Facilities for the examination of information should be established – that has not been done o A register of environmental information should be held by each public body – that certainly has not been done.

And it is not just the Government who have been keen to limit the scope and awareness of AIE. The Directive states that it is 'necessary' for public authorities to disseminate environmental information to the general public to the widest extent possible. The vast bulk of public authorities in Ireland have, perhaps unsurprisingly, been very reluctant to be proactive in this area. Few, if any, have taken the initiative by publicly appointing designated officers, creating registers of information or even mentioning AIE on their websites, just in case someone might make an application!

So the aims of the Directive as outlined in the European version, which is to allow every citizen to have the exact same laws and rights no matter where they live, have not made it into Irish law.

In the original EU Directive there is a presumption of release with paragraph 16 stating that authorities should be permitted to refuse a request only in specific and clearly defined cases. The grounds for refusal, it goes on, should be interpreted in a restrictive way. Ireland's approach, as we've seen, has been less than enthusiastic and in fact has been completely underwhelming with mandatory exemptions and a wider range of discretionary exemptions than in the original document.

Despite all this, AIE still has major potential to allow people access to State information that is not made readily available. It is up to the citizens of Ireland to use it. Even if only to prove a point people should use AIE to make organisations aware of the fact it does exist, citizens know it does exist and citizens know State bodies have obligations under it.

So what is accessible under AIE? Well, an awful lot is the simple answer – although not as much as there should be under the EU version. The important part of the regulations is that there is a very broad definition of what environmental information actually is and it's relatively easy to get.

Article (3)

Article (3)(1) is a crucial part of the regulations as it outlines what information can be sought and who it can be sought from. It covers information in written, visual, aural, electronic or any other form.

- o (1)(a) defines in general what physical aspects of the environment are covered by AIE. They are 'the state of the elements of the environment such as air and atmosphere, water, soil, land, landscape and natural sites including wetlands, coastal and marine areas, biological diversity and its components, including genetically modified organisms and the interaction among these elements.'

- o (b) lists a range of activities which could impact on the environment and are covered by AIE. They are 'factors, such as substances, energy, noise, radiation or waste, including radioactive waste, emissions, discharges and other releases into the environment, affecting or likely to affect the elements of the environment'.

- o (c) relates to plans or works which also fall under AIE. They are 'measures (including administrative measures), such as policies, legislation, plans, programmes, environmental agreements, and activities affecting of likely to affect the elements referred to in paragraph (a) and (b) as well as measures or activities designed to protect those elements'.

- o (d) covers updates on environmental laws planned or active. It states that 'reports on the implementation of environmental legislation' are covered.

o (e) states that financial and economic assessments are also covered; 'cost benefit and other economic analyses and assumptions used within the framework of the measures and activities referred to in paragraph (c)'.

o (f) has a very broad approach to what it covers and is wide open to various interpretations. It states that the Directive also covers 'the state of human health and safety, including the contamination of the food chain, where relevant, conditions of human life, cultural sites and built structures inasmuch as they are, or may be, affected by the state of the elements of the environment referred to in paragraph (a) or through the elements, by any of the matters referred to in paragraphs (b) and (c)'. Only decisions over time by the Commissioner, the High Court and the Supreme Court will give finality to how this section is interpreted.

Due to its lack of use in Ireland, very few decisions have been made by the Commissioner for Environmental Information which would establish precedents. In the UK, where the Directive has been in force longer than here and has more users, the Information Commissioner's Office (ICO) who, like his Irish counterpart, is also responsible for regulating the use of the Directive, has had more decisions to make which we can refer to. The office has also produced a guide to using the Directive which contains some useful definitions. However, British interpretation and decisions, while useful, are no guarantee that the Irish Commissioner for Environmental Information will come to similar conclusions. The laws in Ireland are different and so too is the Irish regulation which gives force to the Directive here. Having said that, there certainly are interesting points contained in the UK interpretation of the Directive.

In relation to (a), the UK Commissioner has said that the information relates not only to current conditions but includes past and predicted future conditions in the environment. The phrase 'such as' means that the list of components is just an example, that the difference between air and atmosphere 'suggests' that air in buildings such as air conditioning could come under the remit of the Regulations. Water in all its forms and in all possible settings (such as natural or man-made systems) is included under AIE.

The Scottish Information Commissioner's guide to AIE also states that 'land' includes material on the surface of the earth but also 'land under the surface'. Land has been described as all land surfaces, buildings, land covered by water and underground strata. By including underground strata the implication is that land also includes natural minerals and deposits such as salt, coal, limestone, slate, iron etc.

Landscape is defined in the European Landscape Convention 2000 as 'an area, as perceived by people, whose character is the result of the action and interaction of natural and/or human factors'. The Scottish Commissioner's guide to AIE goes on to say that a 'specialist environmental definition of landscape is the traits, patterns and structure of a specific geographic area, including its biological composition, its physical environment and its anthropogenic or social patterns'.

Both Commissioners agree that the phrase 'natural sites' includes not just areas designated for specific reasons. It includes 'all sites that are recognised as examples of the landscape in its natural condition, or as sites supporting natural flora or fauna would qualify, including wetlands, coastal and marine areas', according to the ICO reference guide of the environmental regulations.

In relation to paragraph (b), the ICO defines a factor as 'something physical that has an impact or influence' and gives examples such as water being a factor in flooding. However, information about the factor is not necessarily environmental information unless it affects or is likely to affect a component of the environment. On the positive side, the phrase 'likely to affect' sets a low threshold but 'it must be more substantial than a remote possibility' according to the ICO.

Substances includes all material and matter, either natural or synthetic, and includes chemicals, pharmaceuticals, hormones, antibiotics, oil, gasses and liquids according to the ICO, while energy includes thermal, chemical, electrical, kinetic, potential and gravitational, as well as energy like heat, solar energy, sunlight and windpower.

Another interesting definition includes 'radioactive waste', which is not limited to just the stuff which comes from nuclear power stations but can include material produced in hospitals, universities, pharmaceutical industries and research establishments. The words 'emissions' and 'discharges' suggest an accidental or deliberate release of substances, of heat, radiation or noise into air, water or land.

In relation to sub-article (c), the ICO guidelines point that although administrative measures are specifically mentioned, the interpretation of the word 'measures' is not restricted to information of an administrative nature. Measures would include regulatory, economic and voluntary undertakings such as new laws, 'taxes, prosecutions, charges and voluntary agreements. Policies are not restricted to environmental policies but will also take into account development, economic, transport, health and other polices if they are likely to affect the environment'.

Sub-article (d) covers any and all reports or records relating to the monitoring or performance, success or failure of environmental legislation. The European Commission said environmental legislation is 'legislation which, irrespective of its legal basis, contributes to the pursuit of the objectives of . . . policy on the environment . . .

preserving, protecting and improving the quality of the environment, protecting human health, the prudent and rational utilisation of natural resources, and promoting measures at international level to deal with regional or worldwide environmental problems . . .'

Sub-article (e) is closely associated with sub-article (c) and emphasises that as well as economic analysis and cost-benefit studies, the assumptions on which they are based are also subject to AIE.

While all the other subsections are relatively straightforward, subsection (f) can be viewed in several ways. It could mean that it covers almost everything relating to 'the state of human health and safety' with all the areas mentioned afterwards just as an example of areas that are covered by AIE. Or could it be it's the state of human health and safety only in relation to the areas mentioned afterwards? Or is it the state of human health and safety 'inasmuch as they are or may be affected by' the environment? Only when people take appeals to the Commissioner's office will issues like these be finalised.

In the UK, the Information Commissioner's Office has examined this sub-article closely and come to the conclusion that it can be broken down into two main areas. The first is the state of human health and safety, and secondly, the state of cultural sites and built structures. However, it is only when either are or may be affected by the state of the elements of the environment, directly or indirectly, or where they could affect the elements of the environment, can the information be classed as falling under the remit of AIE.

The UK Commissioner has also said 'conditions of human life' will cover, for example, 'information on housing, poverty, employment, social welfare, heating, access to clean water, sanitation and healthcare where these are or may be affected by the environment'. Cultural sites will include places with a historical, literary, educational or artistic value, as well as religious, ethnic or social significance. It covers modern as well as historical sites regardless of location.

The reference to built structures would include roads, railways, pylons, bridges canals and tunnels. It is, however, also arguable that a built structure goes far beyond this definition. Could it, for example, cover much smaller things like cars or buses? They are built, they are structures (within the wider meaning of the word) so information how they impact on the environment or how the environment impacts on them could be subject to AIE.

The Aarhus implementation guide described built structures as man-made constructions which could indeed cover things like cars and buses. The qualification in this sub-article – 'are or may be affected by the state of the elements' – is not as demanding as in the earlier sub-articles. The ICO analysis states that to meet the criteria here 'as long as some link is indicated, there need only be a possibility of an effect occurring'.

Unlike the Freedom of Information Act, when drafting the Directive areas like these were deliberately left vague and open for interpretation so the member state could adopt as open an approach as they wanted. Time will tell just how open Ireland will be in its interpretation.

Also, unlike the FOI Act, Article 3 of the Directive clearly states that it applies to all 'public authorities' which – potentially – covers a vast range of organisations in Ireland. It includes a Minister and their department, the Commissioners of Public Works, every local authority, every harbour authority or State-owned port company, the Health Service Executive, any board or body set up by the Government, a company in which all the shares are held by a Minister or directors appointed by a Minister, and a company which has 'public administrative functions and responsibilities and possessing environmental information'.

This covers a massive range of organisations including all commercial semi-state companies, all of which are exempt from FOI, such as Irish Rail, Bus Éireann, Bord Gais, Bord na Mona, Coillte and the companies in charge of our airports, to mention just a few. Even more interestingly, financial bodies such as the National Treasury Management Agency and all nationalised banks would seem to fall under the remit of AIE – but only in relation to environmental information. Whether the bodies themselves agree or not is irrelevant. A final decision on whether they do or do not rests with the Commissioner for Environmental Regulation, and then, on appeal on a point of law, to the Courts.

No definitive list of public bodies which are subject to AIE has been drawn up by the public body responsible for the implementation of the regulation, the Department of the Environment. Whether this is an accidental oversight or a deliberate decision is not clear, but given the unenthusiastic welcome for AIE it is probably a safe bet that this is no oversight. Most public bodies would, at the very least, be aware of AIE and the fact that they could be subject to requests made under it. However, it seems that most are keen not to promote it.

It is important to note, however, that AIE does not apply to bodies when they are acting in a judicial or legislative capacity. This could, for example, exempt Government departments when they are drafting new laws or the Courts Service in relation to court cases.

In a very significant decision in September of 2011, the Environmental Commissioner has ruled that NAMA is a public body under AIE. This opens up not only this agency but others too which have so far been shielded from scrutiny by the public. Journalist Gavin Sheridan had sought information from the Agency under AIE, but it had refused arguing that it was not a public body. The Commissioner disagreed with the NAMA stance and said they were a public body and therefore subject to AIE.

Article 5

This article discusses the duties of a public authority.

o The authority shall inform the public of their rights under these Regulations and the Directive and provide information and guidance on the exercise of those rights, and

o Make all reasonable efforts to maintain environmental information held by it or for it in a form or manner that is readily reproducible and accessible by information technology or by other electronic means.

Article 6

This goes through the process of formatting a request.

o (1) outlines how to make a request saying it:
  - must be made in writing or electronic form
  - must state the request is made under these Regulations
  - state the name, address and any other relevant contact details of the applicant
  - state, in terms that are as specific as possible, the environmental information that is being requested
  - if the applicant wants the information in a particular form, they must specify that form.

o (2) says that an applicant does not have to say why he or she wants the information.

Article 7

This details what the public authority must do when it receives an AIE request.

o (1) the authority will make available the information requested, subject to law.

o (2)(a) the authority must make a decision on the request as soon as possible but not later than one month.

o (2)(b) where the authority is unable to meet that deadline due to the volume or complexity of the case, they can extend the deadline by a further month after telling the requestor.

o (3)(a) when a request has been made to provide the information in a particular form it should be done unless

- (3)(a)(i) the information is already available in another re-form or

- (3)(a)(ii) giving the information in another form would be more reasonable

o (3)(b) if the information is given in a format different than requested, then the public body must inform the requestor why this is happening

o (4)(a) says that if a decision is made to refuse a request in part or entirely, the body must inform the requestor within a month

o (4)(b) but if this is a complex or voluminous request, then the authority has two months to decide to release or refuse

o (4)(c) the body must specify why the request is being refused

o (4)(d) the requestor must be told of their rights of appeal

o (5) if the request is made to an organisation which does not have the information requested, then the organisation shall inform the requestor as soon as possible that they do not hold it

o (6) if the public authority is aware of which organisation actually holds the information it shall, as soon as possible,

- (6)(a) transfer the request to this other body and inform the requestor or

- (6)(b) tell the requestor which public body holds the information and advise them to contact that body.

Article 8

Here the Irish regulations create exemptions that do not exist in the European Directive. It creates grounds where requests must be refused whereas the European version gives decision makers more freedom by saying that Member States 'may' refuse requests if certain criteria are met. In Ireland this regulation:

- o (1) says that a request can be refused if it would adversely affect:
  - (a)(i) the confidentiality of information about a person who has not consented to it being disclosed
  - (a)(ii) the interests of a person who voluntarily supplied the information being sought
  - (a)(iii) the protection of the environment to which the information sought relates to
  - (a)(iv) the confidentiality of the proceedings of public authorities where that confidentiality is protected by law (including the Freedom of Information Act), or
  - (b) if releasing the records would involve the disclosure of discussions at meetings of the Government.

Article 9

This regulation looks at the area of exemptions.

- o (1) lists the grounds where the deciding officer has discretion to release or refuse if disclosure would adversely affect:
  - international relations, national defence or public security
  - the course of justice (including criminal and disciplinary inquiries)
  - commercial or industrial confidentiality

- intellectual property rights.

o (2) states that public authorities may refuse to release if the request is:
  - manifestly unreasonable in volume or range
  - is formulated in too general a manner
  - concerns material in the course of completion or unfinished
  - relates to internal communications of a public body having considered the public interest.

Article 10

This is an interesting regulation in that it says none of the exemptions can be invoked if certain material is requested.

o (1) none of the above restrictions apply if the information being sought relates to information on emissions into the environment

o (2) states that discussions at Cabinet level are still exempt though

o (3) each request must be considered on an individual basis

o (4) grounds for refusals must be 'interpreted on a restrictive basis having regard to the public interest'

o (5) a body can redact information if it is exempt under Articles 8 and 9

o (6) if a request is refused because the matter sought is not concluded, then the requestor has to be told who is doing it and the estimated completion date

o (7) a non-reply is deemed a refusal.

Article 11

This sets out the appeals mechanism within an organisation. An appeal must be heard by someone unconnected with the original decision and completed within a month.

- o (4) the body must specify the reasons for the refusal or limiting on the release of information being sought and must inform the person of their right of appeal

- o (5) decisions such as the following can be appealed to the Environmental Commissioner:
  - (5)(a) that the organisation contends they are not a public body and therefore not subject to AIE
  - (5)(b) the request has not been adequately answered
  - (5)(c) the request has not been dealt with satisfactorily, including charging excessive fees for photocopying.

Article 12

This regulation states that if the requestor is still unhappy, an appeal can be made to the Commissioner for Environmental Information, but that appeal must be made within a month of the outcome of the internal appeal within the organisation. The Commissioner can uphold, vary or reject the appeal and force the organisation to comply within three weeks.

There is another element to Article 12 that is noteworthy in particular: (3)(a) states that a person who would be affected by a decision to release the information can appeal that decision to the Commissioner. However, this raises an interesting point as there is no part of the Directive or the Irish regulation which gives the public authority the power to inform someone or some company that a request has been made in relation to information that they either supplied, for example, commercially sensitive material or information that affects them in some other way.

If there is no power in the regulation to allow an authority to contact a third party, are they acting outside their powers if they do so? And if a third party is unaware and cannot be told of a potential decision to release, how can they appeal that decision to the Commissioner for Environmental Information?

And even if they are aware of it, they cannot make submissions to the public authority about the matter as there is no provision for this in the regulation. Only if and when the matter gets to the Commissioner can they make a submission – provided they know about it in the first place! This is an issue raised by the Commissioner for Environmental Information, Emily O'Reilly, back in 2008 when she described these problems as 'unusual and perhaps questionable'.

Under this Article, the Commissioner has powers to enter a building and seize any records necessary for an investigation. These are similar to powers that exist under the Freedom of Information Act.

Article 13

This outlines the process for appealing a decision to the High Court – on a point of law only – within two months and, if necessary, then to the Supreme Court.

Article 14

This states that the Minister for the Environment may publish guidelines in relation to how to implement the Regulations and that any public authority then must have regard to them, that is, do what the Minister says. This clearly makes the whole AIE system in Ireland open to political interference or even abuse.

Article 15

This is another example of Ireland's divergence from the spirit of the Directive. The European version states that a 'reasonable' fee may be charged for making records available to cover the costs of photocopying etc. However, sub-article 3 of the Irish Regulations goes on to state that a fee of €150.00 is to be charged for making an appeal to the Commissioner. This is totally against the original aim of the Directive to harmonise laws around the Union for citizens to get information on the environment.

There is a reduced fee of €50.00 for those on medical cards or their dependents. The fee is the same too for a person who may be affected by the decision to release information and who wishes to appeal that decision to the Information Commissioner. This could include personal or commercial reasons, for example.

Summary

So this is, in essence, the Irish regulation which put the European Directive into force in this country. Organisations here will use this when considering requests submitted by citizens, groups or companies. However, because EU law is, in legal terms, superior to Irish law (that is, takes precedence) it is arguably that the EU Directive is the correct version that should be used. The Commissioner herself made reference to this when she said that 'it is important to recognise that the Regulations do not stand alone; they cannot be interpreted outside of the underlying Directive to which they are intended to give effect'. In essence, she said, we must be aware of what the original Directive set out to do. And this is important because it has the potential to open up many of the areas the Irish regulation sought to close off, removing the limits imposed here and giving a freer reign to the idea of accessing information.

It will only be when more appeals are decided by the Commissioner and, inevitably, by the courts will it be really become known just which will win out – the regulation or the Directive. Given all that, it is important that we now look at the original Directive and see how if varies from the Irish regulations in detail.

In the definitions of what is environmental information the Irish regulation matches word for word the European Directive. In fact, Article 3(3) of the Regulations state that if there are words or expressions used in both the Irish Regulations and the European Directive, then the meaning of it should be interpreted from the Directive. Essentially, if there are two ways of looking at a particular element of AIE, then the European view should prevail. However, later on in the same Article, some important pieces of the European Directive are missing from the Irish regulation.

Article 3(5) states that 'member states shall ensure that:

o   Officials are required to support the public in seeking access to information

o   Lists of public authorities are publicly accessible, and

o   The practical arrangements are defined for ensuring that the right of access to environmental information can be effectively exercised such as:
    • the designation of information officers
    • the establishment and maintenance of facilities for the examination of the information required
    • registers or lists of the environmental information held by public authorities or information points with clear indications of where such information can be found.

'Member States shall ensure that public authorities inform the public adequately of the rights they enjoy as a

> result of this Directive and to an appropriate extent pro-
> vide information, guidance and advice to this end.'

The only part of any of that which has happened in Ireland is (a) where officials are required to assist people seeking information. The rest does not appear in the Irish regulation and therefore no organisation or State body will introduce them.

There is no legal reason for this omission, nor would there be a huge cost factor which proves, in my view, that it's not about the money – it's about the access! The decision to omit all of these requirements is clearly not in the interests of the public or the environment. But it is in the interests of the State and its organisations as they can continue without being subject to external scrutiny through AIE – a particularly welcome move from the viewpoint of the organisations and companies which are exempt from FOI but would come under AIE.

Since so many people are aware of FOI and use it, many Government websites and State bodies have links to FOI information on their home pages. There are none with links to AIE on their home page. Some, but not many, do have details of AIE on their website but it takes a bit of searching to find it.

On the issue of exemptions from AIE, the EU Directive is quite specific – but the Irish regulation goes further. Article 4(1) of the Directive only says that member states 'may' provide for a request to be refused if:

o the body does not hold the information sought

o the request is unreasonable

o the request is too vague

o it concerns material in the course of completion or unfinished documents o   relates to internal communications, taking into account the public interest.

Article 4(2) also says requests can be refused if it would adversely affect:

o   the confidentiality of proceedings which are normally protected by law

o   international relations, public security or national defence

o   the course of justice and the ability for a fair trial or hearing

o   the confidentiality of commercial or industrial information, including legitimate economic interests, statistical information and tax matters

o   intellectual property rights

o   confidentiality of personal information

o   the confidentiality of someone or organisation who provided information in confidence

o   and the protection of the environment to which the information relates, such as the location of rare species.

The Directive goes on to say that all these grounds should be interpreted 'in a restrictive way' taking the public interest into account. There are no mandatory exemptions in the EU Directive – this is important.

The Irish regulation, however, introduced mandatory exemptions saying a public authority 'shall not' make available information if it would adversely affect the confidentiality of personal information, 'the interests' (although that is not defined) of a person who voluntarily supplies information, the protection of the environment to which the information relates or the confidentiality of proceedings and discussions at Cabinet.

There is an obvious clash here. If a person requests information and according to the EU version it should be released but is instead refused because of the mandatory exemptions here, then where stands the matter in Irish law? Only legal action here and possibly in Europe can resolve that issue with any finality.

Then once again there's the decision here to impose fees for appeals to the Environmental Commissioner of €150 which is not backed up anywhere in the Directive, and which also seems to be somewhat questionable on a legal basis.

Article 7 of the Directive is entitled 'Dissemination of Environmental Information' and has no counterpart in the Irish regulation. It simply was not transposed into Irish law and has been effectively ignored. It declares that member states 'shall take all necessary measures' to ensure that public authorities organise environmental information with a view to its 'active and systematic dissemination to the public'. It goes on to say that member states 'shall ensure' that environmental information becomes more progressively available and shall include, at the very least, the following under sub-article 2:

o   texts of treaties, agreements and legislation

o   policies, plans and programmes

o   progress reports on implementation

o   reports on the state of the environment

o   data or summaries derived from monitoring activities

o   authorisations with significant impact on the environment. and

o   environmental impact studies and risk assessments on projects.

By not putting the above in the regulation public authorities in Ireland that are subject to AIE do not have to take any action to comply with it. They are not required to publish information so it can only be accessed by AIE. Again, the failure to include this Article is questionable.

It seems clear that what exists in Irish law relating to the Directive only shows how entrenched and regressive the State actually is and how far we still have to go in terms of openness and transparency.

7

Making a Submission under AIE

S O HOW DOES AIE WORK IN REALITY? As we have seen, the answer is not as well as it should because of the restrictions
placed on it here, but even taking these into account it does still
have much to offer. However, there are a number of hurdles to
overcome.

Although it may seem obvious, the first thing you have to determine is what information you want. This may sound easy, but
depending on what you're looking for it could actually be somewhat complex. It is best to write out what you are trying to achieve
and then work back to figure out how to get the result you're seeking. And remember, AIE is about accessing information on the environment. Even with a loose interpretation of the regulation, the
records you seek have fit into some of the criteria laid out in the
previous chapter.

The next step is establishing which State body or bodies are
likely to hold the information you're looking for. Unlike FOI, where
the list of organisations that are subject to the Act can easily be established, either from the Information Commissioner's website or
the body's own website, it is not that straight forward under AIE.

Since the State here has failed to implement the Directive fully,
there is no definitive list of what bodies fall under the remit of the
regulation here. In fact, in a report to the European Commission on

the implementation of AIE in Ireland, the Department of the Environment, which is responsible for the regulation in this country said, 'there is no exhaustive list of the public authorities to which the Regulations apply . . . and it would not be practical to compile such a list'. This statement alone shows how the State has, once again, failed to properly embrace openness and accountability.

But this should not deter you – it should in fact spur you on. All of the bodies which are subject to FOI also fall under the remit of AIE as they are State organisations or State-funded bodies. If they are likely to hold the information you want, then you need to decide under which you wish to make the application. Both have their advantages and disadvantages. For example, FOI covers fewer organisations but offers broader ranger of material that can be sought, whereas AIE is free (up to external appeal level) and there are fewer exemptions allowed, but the request parameters are more limited.

But what if the body which is likely to hold the information is not subject to FOI? Then you need to establish that they are subject to the AIE regime. Once again, that is easier said than done. You could rummage through their website or enter 'Accessing Information on the Environment' or 'AIE' on their internal search engines to see what comes up. They might have a section detailing their approach to FOI and AIE requests. However, if that draws a blank then the next option is to refer to the criteria laid out by the regulation in the previous chapter and see if the body fits into one of these. Does it fulfil the duties of a 'public authority' such as managing a national resource for the benefit of the State or the Government, or are the shares held by a Minister, or by directors appointed by a Minister, and so on? Remember, these are just examples and the range of organisations subject to AIE is much wider.

It is important to note that any firm or contractor working on behalf of an organisation which is subject to AIE is also subject to the Regulation. This could include, for example, companies involved in public–private partnerships or similar projects but only if the work they're doing falls under the description of environmental information.

It is interesting to note too that the Department of the Environment has very limited information about the regulation on its website and really only discusses it in relation to the Department itself. It seems to largely ignore the fact far more organisations than the Department are covered by AIE. This, I believe, is not an oversight. In a review carried out for the European Commission on how AIE was operating in Ireland, the Department only asked other Departments and local authorities about how their views on it – ignoring the many, many other bodies which are subject to AIE.

Once you have established that the organisation is likely to be subject to AIE then you have to write the request. If more than one body may hold the information then you should send separate requests to each of them.

Writing the request is relatively straightforward. Firstly the request can be made by either letter or e-mail to the organisation, although requests in England, Scotland and Wales can be made simply over the phone or even via Twitter. Unlike FOI, there is no application fee. AIE is free until an appeal has to be made to the Environmental Commissioner.

In your letter or e-mail you must state that the request is being made under the Access to Information on the Environment Regulations, give your name, address (email, home or office) and other contact details like mobile phone number. You must then state what environmental information you want and in what format you want it (for example, paper or electronic). You do not have to say why you want the information. Including an e-mail address and a mobile number is important. If someone in the organisation wishes to get in touch to clarify something then it is easier and quicker to do it using either of them rather than by post. You should be as specific as possible in framing the request but not so strict as to eliminate information that may be of use.

Now that's done you face a major hurdle. Who to send the request to? Again, this is a problem created by Ireland's failure to fully transpose the EU Directive into Irish law.

Sub-article 5 of Article 3 in the EU version states that (a) officials are required to support the public in seeking to access information, (b) lists of public authorities are publicly accessible and (c) practical arrangements are in place to make it easy for citizens to get the information by designating information officers, establishing facilities for examining files and creating lists of the environmental information held by a public authority or creating information points with indications of where the information can be found.

None of this exists in the Irish version, which appears to be a deliberate omission. In any case, the effects are pretty clear. The Irish version makes it more awkward to establish which organisations are subject to AIE, and then to identify the person within that organisation to contact when requesting information.

Even the office of the Environmental Commissioner does not have a complete list of bodies which would be subject to AIE. In a letter to the Department of Finance in September 2009, the Commissioner's office sought a list of all organisations the Department had sent a circular to relating to the use of AIE regulations.

In that same letter the Commissioner highlighted several problems with the transposition of the Directive, including confusion as to who is the contact person within an organisation for receiving requests.

> 'In many cases, it appears that no-one has been designated to co-ordinate the process and there is no guarantee that an application made under the Regulations will be dealt with in accordance with articles 7–9.'

So how do you find out who to send the request to? In bodies which are subject to FOI there is usually a link on their webpage so you could send your AIE request to the address given for FOI requests. You should make it clear, however, that the request is being made under the Access to Information on the Environment Regulations.

It gets tricky, however, in relation to bodies that are not subject to FOI. Some of the staff there may be aware of AIE and the fact that the body is subject to it but, as AIE is still relatively unknown, chances are many of the employees will know little about the body's duty under the Regulations. The added difficulty is that such bodies are not used to dealing with AIE and the requirements it places on them in terms of answering requests.

So how do you find a contact person for requests when no one has been designated? The best way is to phone the organisation and ask if there is a person dealing with AIE requests. If there is, get their name and e-mail address. If there's not, then probably the best way is to ask for their public affairs office, get an e-mail address and send the request there. Make sure to mention in your e-mail that you would like an acknowledgement that your request has been received.

If you have no success with either approach, then most organisations have a general e-mail contact address so send the request there with the same polite requirement for an acknowledgement. You could also post a letter, hand deliver it, send one by registered post or just keep phoning until someone answers and is willing to receive your request. This is all very unsatisfactory and means that many requestors will give up at the first hurdle.

Hopefully, however, someone from the organisation will get back to you and the request can proceed. But if you hear nothing back from the initial request you should send the e-mail every week for a month with a warning that you will follow the matter up with the Environmental Commissioner if there is no response. And if there is no response then you should appeal this 'non-decision' to the Commissioner's office, but that's going to cost €150.00.

But presuming that the body has received and acknowledged the request, they then have one month to decide whether to release or deny access to all or part of the information. If the request is particularly large or complex, then the body can extend this 'deciding time' by a further month, but only after informing you first. There's no part of the regulation that allow you to object to that extension.

If it transpires that the information you seek is actually held by another organisation, then the body to whom you made the request must either inform you of the identity of that other organisation or transfer your request to them.

If your request is ambiguous, the organisation must contact you and try to narrow down the scope of what you're seeking before they can refuse on grounds that the request is too vague.

If the organisation decides to refuse the request either in part or in totality, they must inform you and specify the reason for the refusal as well as inform you of your rights of appeal.

This has also been a problem area according to the Commissioner for Environmental Information. In communications with the Department of Environment, the Commissioner highlighted several cases where requestors had not been informed of the time limits that exist in AIE or of rights to appeal decisions. In one case, a Government department claimed to have carried out an internal review, the result of which was that the issue should be sent back to the original deciding officer to have another look at the case! This shows either a complete lack of understanding of AIE or a complete unwillingness to implement it correctly. The proper approach is for the appeal to be considered by a higher grade civil servant looking at the issue independently and making up their own mind on whether to release or refuse.

The authority may also try to convince you that they are not subject to AIE, but if they meet any of the criteria laid down in the Directive and regulation then they are! The organisation may also try to fob you off with a partial release saying that's all they have on the particular matter.

Unfortunately, this too is a problem that the Commissioner has encountered on more than one occasion. Several times requestors have been told that the records they seek are not environmental information though they clearly are, while in other cases the public body claimed that no records of the type being sought actually exist. Subsequently, when the Commissioner's office got involved considerable volumes of records were identified.

In one published decision, Kildare County Council informed an applicant that it held no records relating to his request for information about the construction of a new sewer. There was an internal appeal and that decision was affirmed. When the requestor lodged an appeal to the Environmental Commissioner, the Council changed its mind and found a lot of documents – 53 files worth of material in fact! As part of the appeal, the Commissioner got the Council to contact two outside contractors who worked on the project and that turned up another 30 files.

In dealing with separate cases, the Commissioner has also gone as far as saying that some public authorities have adopted 'a defensive and unhelpful' attitude in dealing with certain requestors because of previous contacts between them, which is clearly not in the spirit of AIE.

Refusals – legitimate or otherwise – are inevitable. In some cases the authority will be correct, but not in all. Regardless, the first thing you need to do if not being granted full access to the information is to get the refusal in writing, either by e-mail or by let-ter. That should state the specific part or parts of the regulation being cited to prevent or limit release.

Like FOI, there is a pathway to follow afterwards. The first step is to seek an internal appeal. Information about this and who to appeal to should be included in the letter outlining the decision of the authority in response to your request. If it is not, ask the person who made the initial decision who you can contact for an internal appeal.

Writing an appeal under AIE is similar to an appeal under FOI. The best approach is to address each of the issues raised by the au-thority in their letter limiting or refusing you access to the informa-tion. Remember, there are fewer exemptions in AIE and almost all are subject to a public interest test.

Once again, the issue of lack of awareness or lack of openness is something that features in appeals. The Environmental Commis-sioner has said that the grounds for the refusal put forward by many organisations are wrong, which highlights the problems with understanding or appreciating the scope of AIE. The simple mes-sage remains: do not be put off if your request has been refused – appeal!

A request to Kildare County Council for details about the in-stallation of a sewer across the River Liffey at Leixlip by John Col-gan was rejected in its entirety. The Council had argued that it did not hold any environmental information within the scope of the request. The matter was appealed to the Commissioner and as a result the Council did release some information. The Commis-sioner's office, however, found the Council to be less than forth-coming and had to force them to release other information.

> *A request was made to RTÉ seeking information, amongst other things, about the environmental qualifications of a number of staff as well as the criteria used by the company to assess issues such as environmental hazard. RTÉ turned down the request on a variety of grounds, including that it believed it was not a public body subject to the regulation. By the time the matter was appealed to the Office of the Commissioner for Environmental Information RTÉ accepted that it was a body subject to the regulation but again rejected the request. The Commissioner upheld RTÉ's decision.*

The public interest test seems to be another problem for those dealing with AIE requests. According to the Commissioner, there seems to be little evidence of deciding officers taking the public interest into account, judging from the appeals that are being lodged to her office. Even when the test has been brought to the notice of the organisation it has just been ignored in some cases.

> *When a member of Wicklow County Council, Tommy Cullen, sought copies of records held by the Department of the Environment primarily in relation to illegal dumping, some were released but others were not. In her review, the Commissioner was critical of the Department for failing to consider the public interest in releasing the information which had been sought. She ordered the Department to release most of the records it had withheld.*

These problems will not go away as long as AIE remains underutilised. The more people use the Regulations and understand what they are entitled to, the more the State organisations will come to the realisation that they have obligations and that citizens have rights.

In making out appeals it is worth spending time developing arguments as to why the organisation was wrong to limit or refuse to release the information. With the exception, that is, of requests refused under Article 8. In this Article the Irish authorities claim the exemptions are mandatory so you will need to prepare for an appeal to the Environmental Commissioner. You must formally go through the process of making an internal appeal, but any internal appeal relating to Article 8 will automatically be turned down. The only option then is either to give up or appeal to the Commissioner.

The Irish regulation has created an obvious conflict regarding 'mandatory' exemptions which does not exist in the European Directive. Article 8 lists a series of records which are exempt 'subject to Article 10'. That would seem to give Article 10 more power than Article 8, but that depends on the decision makers' definition of 'subject' and 'mandatory'.

Article 8(1) states that a public body 'shall not' make environmental information available if it would adversely affect (a) the confidentiality of information about a person who has not consented to it being released; (b) the interests of a person who volunteered information 'unless that person has consented to the release of that information'; (c) the protection of the environment to which the records relate; and (d) confidentiality of proceedings of public authorities. Article 8(2) covers records which would reveal what was said at Cabinet.

Importantly, Article 10 states that none of the above exemptions – with the exception of Cabinet confidentiality – apply but only if the records being sought relate to emissions into the environment.

In making any appeal, you should query every aspect of the decision to refuse. Trying to overturn a 'mandatory' decision to refuse to release under Article 8 is not easy but it is not impossible either!

In a historic decision in October 2008, the Environmental Commissioner decided that information which related to emissions should be released even though it would reveal comments which were made at Cabinet. Although the decision was overturned on appeal to the High Court, the matter can only be finalised by the Supreme Court or even the European Court of Justice.

The importance of the Commissioner's decision in this case is that it shoots down the idea of Ireland's 'mandatory exemptions', and even if it is only limited to the area of emissions, it provides an important first step which can slowly be expanded upon.

In this case, Gary Fitzgerald sought records which reported Cabinet discussions on Ireland's greenhouse gas emissions between the years 2002 and 2007. Although some records were released, others were not, including one which included notes of a conversation at Cabinet. On appeal, the Environmental Commissioner found that the 'Cabinet exemption' does not conform with the original EU Directive. The Department of the Taoiseach argued that the Commissioner was bound by the Irish regulation, but she said she could not ignore a situation where this regulation was in conflict with the Directive.

In relation to the other exemptions claimed under Article 8, it is a requirement that there be some 'adverse affect' before the exemption can be used. What this means is that the public authority must be able to prove disclosure would 'adversely affect' someone or some organisation.

In the guidance notes issued by the UK Information Commissioner in relation to this issue, they state that 'adversely affect' means that some harm is probable – not just likely – if records are released. Merely believing or suggesting that harm could occur is not enough. Harm must be likely to occur. This is the first and not insignificant hurdle for the public body to prove.

In relation to confidentiality of personal information, Article 8(a)(i), it is common practice to protect such data from general release, although the Irish regulation make this mandatory whereas the original Directive stated it 'may' exclude from release. While there is nothing in the regulation to say a public body can contact someone if a request has been made for personal information about them, it would only be fair to contact the person whose information is being sought and let them know. It could be that the person supplied information about a breach of the law or other serious issues so it would make sense that they would be offered protection by the regulation.

But what is 'personal information'? The clearest definition is defined as data which relates to a living individual who can be identified from it either directly or indirectly. It is possible to argue that removing some information from a record would eliminate the possibility of the person being identified, leaving the remainder of the record available for release. It is also a requirement that the authority must be able to prove an 'adverse affect' is likely. Just because a document contains information about a person that does not automatically exclude it from release.

In relation to Article 8(a)(ii), protecting the 'interests' of someone who volunteered information, it is again generally accepted that if someone supplied important information on the understanding that their identity would remain confidential it would be proper that the person would be entitled to have that honoured. As well as clearly identifying an adverse effect, the public body should also be clearly able to define how it would not be in this person's interest to have the information released. Just because they say it would not be in the person's interest does not make it a reality.

In relation to Article 8(a)(iii), 'protection of the environment', it would clearly be counterproductive to release information about a part of the environment which could actually lead to damage being done to it. For example, if a rare species bird or flower or a unique archaeological site were found releasing information about its exact whereabouts could bring an influx of visitors who could cause harm. A counter-argument in an appeal could again focus on the issue of adverse effect and that it's not just a possibility but a probability that harm would be done before it can be invoked.

Article 8(a)(iv), 'confidentiality of proceedings of public authorities', has the potential to be quite powerful in limiting the scope of information which could be released. It is important to note that this confidentiality extends to information which is already protected by other laws. Of particular concern here is the specific inclusion of the Freedom of Information Act.

While the regulation provides for more openness and transparency in many regards than FOI, the State however has tried to limit that openness by saying that only information on the proceedings of public authorities which could be released under FOI can be released under AIE.

An appeal to the Commissioner over this sub-Article should point out that the original EU Directive only said such exemptions 'may' apply and not the overly restrictive 'shall' apply as the State has introduced here; point out that wide scope of this exemption is not mirrored in the original EU Directive; focus in on the adverse affect necessary for exemption because if there is none or if it seems tenuous then the public body cannot correctly claim it is exempt under this Article.

It is also worth noting that in an AIE decision, Cullen & The Department of the Environment, Heritage and Local Government, the Commissioner looked at the issue of confidentiality of proceedings of public bodies. In making her decision, she cited a 1984 High

Court case where the judge said there are three elements to a breach of confidence:

> '. . . first, the information itself . . .must have the necessary quality of confidence about it. Secondly, that information must have been imparted in circumstances imposing an obligation of confidence. Thirdly, there must be an unauthorized use of that information to the detriment of the party communicating it.'

If the records being sought do not meet any of those criteria, this exemption cannot be invoked and which is a point worth considering.

The Environmental Commissioner has ruled that the area of legal professional privilege falls under Article 8(a)(iv) too. This privilege covers two areas: communications between a client and legal advisor giving legal advice, and legal communication which is related to pending litigation. Although this is subject to a public interest test, the Commissioner has found that there would have to be 'exceptional' public interest reasons to overturn this exemption.

Article 8(b) is the exemption which prevents the disclosure of discussions of the Government. As there is no mention of the Freedom of Information Act here it is possible that Government really means Cabinet and does not include the vast extension granted under the 2003 amendment of the FOI Act although that matter can only be finalised by appeals to the Commissioner and probably the courts. Article 28 of the Irish Constitution prevents the release of information which would reveal what was said at Cabinet and it would seem that this is the most iron-clad exemption. As we've seen, however, it is not. Although the Commissioner's decision was overturned by the High Court, the matter will only be finalised when the Supreme Court and possibly the European Court of Justice decide on the issue.

If the request is refused under Article 9 where the decision maker has discretion you must, like under FOI, make a good case as to why the original decision to refuse or limit the release was incorrect. It is unlikely that if the records sought would genuinely cause the sort of harm as listed out in sub-article (1) that they would be released either on application or on appeal. However, never presume that an exemption has been properly applied to a record or piece of information.

When it has been done incorrectly it does not necessarily mean that the public body deliberately tried to hide something using the wrong sub-article. It is more likely that the deciding officer believed that the material was exempt, and believing that the worst possible outcome is always inevitable, made the incorrect decision to limit or refuse release.

Some possible arguments which could be made against a refusal or limited release under Article 9(1)(a) where release would harm international relations, national defence or public security could include:

o The information being sought would or could not do the harm envisaged and/or

o Public security is best served by releasing the information you seek but be prepared to back this up with a reasoned argument

o Since all other countries in the EU are subject to AIE that similar requests to other countries would be likely to illicit similar or identical information anyway

o That the deciding officer failed to give due consideration to the public interest and then outline why there is such significant public interest in the information you're seeking

o That the deciding office failed to consider Article 10(4) that grounds for refusing must be interpreted on a restrictive basis o The claim of 'adverse affect' is not backed up by a strong and credible argument.

Under Article 9(1)(b), 'the course of justice', legal information that would be exempt under FOI such as communications between a legal advisor and a client are likely to be exempted here too. However, remember that just because an exemption is claimed that does not mean it is claimed properly.

Even under Article 9(1)(c), 'commercial or industrial confidentiality', an organisation cannot refuse to release information about emissions. If the exemption is to be used, it must only be used to protect a 'legitimate economic interest'. Again, while there is a lack of precedence in Ireland, decisions on the similar exemption under the Freedom of Information Act are likely to form the basis of rulings under AIE.

To claim an exemption under Article 9(1)(d), 'intellectual property rights', it must only cover rights which were granted to creators and owners or works that are the result of human intellectual creativity. It could include artistic work or patents and trademarks, for example, but this is not an exhaustive list. The public body must be able to show that releasing information under this sub-Article would cause adverse harm, that is, undermine the rights of those who own them.

In relation to Article 9(2)(a) which covers requests that are 'manifestly unreasonable', decision makers can consider the volume or the range of information being sought. While there are no cost limits imposed under AIE, if a request is simply too large it can be refused. Appealing a decision to refuse which cites this sub-Article, you would have to make a good argument that while it may be a large request, there is a strong public interest case in making the information available.

There is no definition of what is a 'manifestly unreasonable' request under AIE in Ireland and it is very much an individual interpretation. Possible examples would be something like requesting information from the gardaí about the number of kilometres driven by each patrol car in the country over the last year, together with the emissions output from each vehicle, or the educational status of everyone in the Department of the Environment. Both these are likely to be seen as 'manifestly unreasonable' requests.

However, in the UK guidance notes regarding AIEs it states that volume and complexity alone are not reasons for refusing to release under this Article, nor is there any limit to the costs that can arise in meeting a request.

Requests which could fairly be seen as obsessive or harassing the organisation or individuals could be judged as unreasonable. Other issues for deciding officers to consider are whether the request seems designed to cause disruption, or does the request 'impose a significant burden in terms of expense and distraction'.

To judge a request as manifestly unreasonable, decision makers should be able to make relatively strong arguments under several of these headings – but not necessarily all.

Before a request can be deemed unreasonable, the organisation must assist you in refining your request so that it cannot be exempted for these reasons. If they do not, then they are in breach of the regulation themselves.

If a request is refused under Article 9(2)(b), that it is formulated 'in too general a manner', it should be possible to rework your request to avoid falling into this exemption. Again, the public authority has to contact you within twenty days of receiving the request to try to resolve the matter. They will discuss what exactly you are looking for (they should not ask you why you are looking for it but if they do you do not have to answer). It could be that what may seem a simple request to you could actually involve tremendous amount of work trawling through files covering a vast array of information. It could be that the deciding officer simply cannot figure out what you are looking for so communication is the best policy here to avoid a refusal. If there is an appeal, you would have to convince the official considering the appeal, and possibly, the Environmental Commissioner, that the request can be met and that there is a public interest in the information being released.

A refusal which cites Article 9(2)(c), 'material in the course of completion', has the potential to offer significant protection to work that is underway within a public body. But when the work is completed, are the records created during that work exempt from release? There are differing views on this. In Ireland draft reports on an issue can be released following a decision in Cullen & the Department of the Environment, Heritage and Local Government. In the UK, the Information Tribunal (where decisions of the Information Commissioner can be appealed) ruled that a draft report will always be a draft report and therefore remains 'material in the course of completion' and so is exempt. Appeals against this exemption here should cite the public interest as a strong reason for releasing the information and query the adverse effect disclosure is likely to create.

A refusal under Article 9(2)(d) 'internal communications', does not have a time limit, that is it does not expire when the issue being discussed has concluded. However, the public interest test is, as always, a strong argument to make in favour of release. This exemption is to allow for what's called 'thinking space' within an organisation while it is decided what or when to do something about an issue or problem. Logically, it would seem that the word 'internal' means this exemption only relates to communications within a body and that communications with another organisation about the same issue should be accessible. However, that's not the view taken in the UK. There the Information Commissioner ruled that this AIE exemption applies to communications between government departments, but does not extend to covering communications between a government department and, for example, a local authority or even between local authorities. That, however, may not be a view shared by the Environmental Commissioner here in Ireland.

In an appeal, the organisation (or organisations) will have to argue that the information being sought is internal and demonstrate what the adverse effect would be of releasing the records.

As noted previously, just like under FOI, the issue of fees is also a problem with AIE. While there are no fees for making requests or seeking internal appeals, there is a fee of €150 to make an appeal to the Environmental Commissioner. There is no mention or provision for such a fee in the original directive. It is another example of the State here trying to put as many people off from making appeals as possible. Don't give in.

8

Freedom of Information and Business

O F THE 15,000 FREEDOM OF INFORMATION requests made in 2010, only six per cent of them were actually submitted by businesses. That shows just how underused FOI and AIE are among the business community.

There are a couple of reasons why both pieces of legislation could be extremely useful to companies. The principle ones relate to: (a) accessing State information to seek out new opportunities; (b) seeking information about tenders; (c) seeking information relating to competitors or (d) seeing what plans or proposals are being formulated which could impact on the company.

There is also a vast reservoir of data that is collected by the very many State bodies but which is largely untapped at the minute. There is no doubt that accessing and reusing this information does have huge commercial potential. In fact, the market here in Ireland alone has been estimated to be worth up to €400 million per year.

So while there are many potential benefits there are, of course, issues of concern for companies which undertake business with State bodies. For example, could competitors access sensitive information about them?

Both the Freedom of Information Act and the regulation on Accessing Information on the Environment have several sections built in to protect such sensitive information, but that does not mean that all information or records about a business deal are exempt from release.

Every year the State in its various forms gathers a huge amount of information which relate to us, the citizens, the country's finances, the environment or technology for example. When you to take into account the considerable number of State organisations and the very different areas they're involved with it is possible to get an idea of the huge amount of information they gather and hold. Multiply that across Europe and then amount and range of information becomes truly staggering. In fact the public sector across the continent is the single largest producer of information.

Most public sector bodies need information to be able to function and to deliver their core responsibilities. For the most part that is as far as the information goes. But there is a huge potential market for either refined or the raw data.

With this in mind, the European Union spent sometime working on a plan to encourage States to open up this information – with protections built in for confidential and personal data.

What emerged was the Directive 2003/98/EC, which led to the formal establishment of PSI (Public Sector Information). Although published in 2003, it was a further two years before it became law in Ireland. It allows for the reuse of information gathered by public sector bodies, and also includes a framework across each EU country giving citizens and businesses equal rights and opportunities to gain access to the data in their own or any country within the EU.

The idea is to encourage the State to make information they already collect accessible at no charge or sold off at a relatively nominal value. As well as having the potential to raise some funds for the body itself, the companies who access that information can develop ways to use it, creating more business opportunities for themselves – and hopefully more jobs.

Of course, the use of the information is not limited to commercial interests. It is equally possible for charities or non-governmental organisations to use the information for their own benefits. There is also the acknowledged indirect benefit that more public access to such information could improve collection methods, analysis and decision making.

The aim of the Directive is to 'stimulate economic activity, innovation and competition and to assist the evolution of an information and knowledge-based economy and society'.

The Department of Finance set up a special website, www. psi.gov.ie, as part of this country's plans to meet its requirements under the Directive. The Regulations, which brought the Directive into Irish law, place an obligation on public sector bodies to provide information about material they are prepared to release (but not necessarily the information itself). There are a wide range of bodies listed on the website, including some of which are outside the remit of the Freedom of Information Act such as the gardaí. There is, however, no sign of other State organisations like the Central Bank or NAMA being listed, which is not surprising given the tendency towards secrecy here.

There are plenty of examples where data collected by State bodies is already available free to all. For instance, Dublin City Council have pictures from many of their CCTV cameras available online, organisations responsible for distributing grants have information available online about the type of grants available and who has received them in the past, and many school inspection reports carried out by the Department of Education are available, to mention just a few.

But even where the information is already available free there are plenty of business opportunities for individuals or companies to collate it from a variety of sources into one single location, for example, a site which lists all possible grants available to community organisations around the country from various public bodies.

And in cases where the information is collected but not published it is possible to access it and then 'data mine' it for further use. For example, insurance companies could use meteorological data or information from local authorities about flooding concerns to refine their premiums for specific areas, business or financial statistics could be explored in more detail by experts, or demographic information could be 'mined' to find out where the highest concentration of a particular age group live for geo-marketing. And it could also be possible to set up a consultancy business which would obtain and refine whatever type of information a particular company or sector was interested in.

As a result of the Directive, Ireland has a standard Public Sector Information Licence, or PSI for short, which is pretty much the same across the EU. It allows for the reuse of information gathered by the public sector but there are certain conditions attached. These conditions state that whoever is reusing public sector information must cite clearly the identity, source, the title and date of publication and where the data came from, including copyright details. The copyright remains with the public sector even if a business reuses it for its own benefits.

The information cannot be used for advertising or promoting a product or service, it cannot be used for illegal, immoral, dishonest purposes, it cannot be used in a way that would imply endorsement by the public sector, it cannot be used in a misleading fashion and the re-user cannot use the crest, logo or mark of the public sector body.

In Ireland, PSI licences cover all central Government departments, local authorities and most non-commercial public sector bodies. However, as well as the exclusion of financial bodies, educational, research, cultural and public service broadcasters are also excluded from having to provide information for reuse.

But while PSI is one path to information there are others, in particular the Freedom of Information Act and the regulation on Accessing Information on the Environment. Business-related Freedom of Information requests have been regularly used to obtain commercially useful information from State bodies. It's not necessarily 'commercially sensitive' information, as that is a lot harder to access under any regulation, but it is information that someone or some company finds useful for their business.

So what's the difference between commercially useful and commercially sensitive? An example of commercially useful could be if a request was put into a State body looking at specific elements of their future plans. The information subsequently released could reveal potential business opportunities. Commercially sensitive information, on the other hand, would be looking for how much competitors are bidding for a contract during an active tendering process.

Following a successful appeal to the Information Commissioner seeking details of a winning bid to provide the army with vehicles, a further application was then made seeking details of the unsuccessful bids. The Commissioner ruled that while the details of the successful bid had been released the details of the unsuccessful ones remained commercially sensitive and should not be released.

The Commissioner said that as a general rule where the confidential or sensitive information of a tenderer does not involve the spending of public money then the public interest generally lies in protecting that information from release.

Business requests to State organisations are likely to be examined through two distinct but linked parts of the Act. The main part of FOI, which gives protection to commercially sensitive information is Section 27 while Section 26 offers protection to information given in confidence, for example, tenders or analyses of companies. Both these sections allow requests seeking information about a commercial business and its work with a State body to be refused.

The other areas which are important for business requests are Section 20, which covers the deliberations of public bodies, and Section 21, which relates to the functions and negotiations of public bodies. These two sections allow, amongst other things, for business-related requests to be refused while matters are being or have been considered within the State body, while negotiations are underway or were conducted with the potential contractor.

Closer examination of Section 27 shows that it allows for an organisation to refuse to release records if they contain trade secrets, information which would result in a financial loss or gain for the person or company which the records relate to, prejudice their competitive position or prejudice negotiations. However, the same section goes on to say that an organisation must release the information if the person to whom it relates consents for its release, if information 'of the same kind' is already available to the public, if the records relate to the person making the request, or if disclosure is necessary to prevent harm to an individual or the environment. There is a public interest clause in this Section which is also very important.

In relation to Section 26 (information given in confidence), several decisions of the Commissioner have relied on certain principles to establish whether the records were given in confidence. The body or the company must be able to prove that the information was given on the understanding it would be treated as confidential, that releasing it would prejudice information being given to that or similar bodies, that it was of sufficient quality and that it was information of such significance that it is important public bodies must continue to able to receive it.

The insertion of 'confidentiality clauses' into agreements does not necessarily mean they will not be exempt from release either. Again, where there is a public interest test, the use of public funds has a strong influence on whether record should be released or not – and generally the decision is to release.

Section 20 is aimed at allowing organisations' 'thinking space' to discuss issues and, amongst other things, examine contracts or possible contractors. There is a public interest clause here which is very important in making appeals. There is another element to Section 20, subsection (2), which states that exemptions do not apply to records used or to be used to make recommendations or decisions, factual information, the reasons for a particular decision or any reports or scientific analysis commissioned for the body. However, Section 20 also offers the potential for Ministerial Certificates to be issued, which exempt information from being released without appeal, regardless of content.

Section 21 relates to protection of information where release could harm the functions or the negotiations of the organisation. The decision maker has discretion whether to release information even if it comes under the influence of this section, and there is a public interest clause here which is always important. For example, this could cover a marking scheme devised within an organisation to select a winning bid for a tender, or it could cover negotiations between the organisation and a company for a specific commercial contract.

Businesses seeking information under FOI use the exact same process as an individual, although remember that a few Government departments put up on their website the details of requests such as the names of companies and journalists and what they're seeking. The identity of individual persons who make FOI requests are not disclosed on the FOI log, although the details of the request may be. The records which are released as a result of the requests are also often put up on the Department's website too for all to see.

But before any company can get that far they have to submit the request to the body along with the €15.00 fee stating what records are being sought. Once the request has been received the official will examine what records are being sought and if they are likely to be exempt from release under FOI, and whether there's another individual or company involved in relation to the information, for example, if they supplied the details to the organisation that are being sought.

If there are, the official will separate the records that contain third party information from the ones that do not. They're likely then to contact the requester and ask if they are actually seeking information relating to the third party. If they are not, then the records are excluded and what remains is considered as per usual.

If they are then the individual or business which supplied the information being sought is contacted to get their views. While these are important, they are not binding on the organisation. It's up to the deciding officer to conclude whether the information can be released or not.

However, the guide for deciding officers adopts a pretty negative approach to releasing information. It states that:

> '. . . even if your initial instinct is very much towards protection of the information, informal contact may be useful. The third party may have supporting views on the applications of the exemption which could serve to reinforce your decision.'

This is all very negative in its attitude. What's wrong with highlighting the aims of FOI and mentioning that exclusions are not supposed to be the norm? The Information Commissioner has found on several occasions that an organisation refused to release information because it was claimed to be 'commercially sensitive' relating to an individual or company. When contacted by the Commissioner's office, however, it emerged the business or person had no objection to information being released!

If the deciding officer takes the view that the information sought is not commercially sensitive nor given in confidence, they may decide to release it. But before they can do that, they have to advise the person or company who supplied the information of their decision. That person or company then has the right to appeal this decision to the Information Commissioner. In doing this they have to make out grounds as to why the original decision to release is wrong and what harm would be caused to them or their business if the records are released.

However, there is still the public interest to consider. There is strong public interest in openness in the use of public funds and ensuring the money is spent properly. The Commissioner has said frequently that the arguments put forward to prevent releasing the information do not meet the necessary standards of proving harm, and so have to be released.

The view, often repeated by the Commissioner, is that openness and accountability of a public body in spending public money 'represents a very strong public interest of release'.

But that doesn't mean information is guaranteed to be released. Since the very first Commissioner was appointed, they have all accepted that there is a legitimate public interest in 'persons being able to conduct commercial transactions with public bodies without fear of suffering commercially as a result'.

The 'harm test' in Section 27 is important here. It does not relate to the actual information itself, but to what harm would be caused by its release. The threshold of proof is pretty low – just that harm might be caused.

Considering the opposite view, how would a company or individual who submitted information to a State body try to prevent it from being released under FOI? Having been informed by the organisation that they have received the request, they'll be invited to make their views known. If the decision to release still stands, they will given an opportunity to appeal the decision to the Information Commissioner before the records are released. In that appeal they must make out an argument that they or their business will suffer as a result of the release. The argument must be convincing enough to sway the Commissioner that harm 'might' result. An appeal should also address the public interest issue, that is, how it would not be in the public interest (the public can be just one person) to release the information.

The issue of accessing information on businesses directly, whether competitors or not, is certainly trickier. For example, if a request was made looking for all records relating to a certain company, which included not only letters or emails between them and a public body but also internal documents created within the State body as officials discussed any issue or problem they may have with that particular firm, once again the issue of commercially sensitive information comes to the fore. If the records sought could reveal concerns about the viability of the business then they are very unlikely to be released, certainly while the business is still trading, although the issue would likely change if the company failed. The records could then be considered historical and therefore have less impact in terms of being commercially sensitive.

If the records sought discussed ongoing problems the State body was having with a particular company or with equipment they supplied, then that too could easily fall under the ambit of commercially sensitive information.

Remember, however, that just because an argument is put forward to refuse the release of documents that does not mean it will stand up to scrutiny by the Information Commissioner. In several cases decisions have been made on appeal to release information, including details of e-mails, phone calls and meetings between officials and companies where commercial transactions were discussed. Once again, the public interest in seeing that public funds are spent properly is a powerful tool in arguing for the release of information that may, on the face of it, seem to be commercially sensitive.

But it is not just 'historical' deals that can be of interest here. FOI also allows companies and individuals to look to the future to try to spot business opportunities arising. For example, when a new strategy is launched it is possible to submit an FOI request seeking access to all the records related to that strategy. This could reveal what options were examined by those who drew up the plan. Did they examine all of them properly? And crucially, is there a potential to develop a business around part or all of it, directly or indirectly?

Looking at how a decision was arrived at, particularly in relation to internal discussions, can often reveal a particular 'thought process' or thread that could potentially offer business opportunities but which never made it into the final report or were not highlighted sufficiently. It could be that the report was not designed as a job creation project, but a keen business eye might spot an opportunity that they could exploit.

Using the Regulations on Access to Information on the Environment can offer a wide range of material from an even wider range of organisations than FOI, but the information must relate, in some way, to the environment. AIE applies to many more bodies than FOI and allows access to commercially useful information from many State and semi-State organisations. Section 3(c) specifically mentions that records relating to measures such as administrative operations, policies, plans programmes and activities are subject to release. Section 3(e) also states that cost benefit and other economic analyses and assumptions can be released on request.

However, as already highlighted, there are several exemptions which could impact on business-related requests. There is the 'mandatory' exemption protecting personal information and the confidentiality of the proceedings of public bodies but there are also discretionary exemptions relating to commercial and industrial confidentiality which are aimed at protecting 'a legitimate economic interest' or intellectual property rights.

These exemptions offer companies security in that they can do business with State and semi-State bodies in the knowledge that commercially sensitive information will be exempt from release. For those seeking records or data there is still plenty of scope to obtain information that would or at least could be commercially useful and, if appealing a decision to the Environmental Commissioner, it is worth querying whether the records really are entitled to exemption.

9

Accessing and Protecting Personal Information

MUCH OF THE AWARENESS OF the Freedom of Information Act is due to the media using it to publish or broadcast stories based on records released to them. For this reason, many politicians and senior civil servants are still somewhat hostile to the Act and, in particular, its use by the media in the belief that it is mainly used to generate controversy and cause embarrassment.

It will probably come as a surprise then to many that journalists only make up around 14 per cent of the overall number of people who make requests under FOI. In fact, the largest single group of requestors are people seeking personal information about themselves. They make up 57 per cent of all requests, according to the 2010 annual report of the Information Commissioner.

In total, there were over 10,500 requests for personal information made during 2010 to various public bodies using the Freedom of Information Act. But this is just a fraction of the overall number of people who request personal information from public and other bodies. Many people use the alternative route of making requests under the Data Protection Act to get personal information. In this chapter we'll look at both pieces of legislation, how to make requests, avoid pitfalls and the relative strengths and weaknesses of each.

Firstly what is 'personal information' or 'personal data'? Under the Data Protection Act, 'personal data' is defined as information relating to a person who is alive who can be identified either:

a) Directly from that information (for example, the records contain their name and address) or

b) Who can be identified by using several pieces of information which the controller of the data either has in their possession or is likely to come into their possession (for example, one record might refer only to a 'Mr. X', who is a target of a tax investigation, while a second record identifies this person but makes no reference to him being the subject of a tax investigation. Taken together, it is very easy to identify who is the subject of this tax probe.)

The EU Data Protection Directive (95/46/EC) has a similar definition of 'personal data'. It defines it as any information relating to 'an identified or identifiable natural person'. An identifiable person is one who can be identified, directly or indirectly, by reference to a specific number (for example, staff number or address) or to one or more factors such as physical, mental, economic, cultural or social identity.

The definition of personal information under the Freedom of Information Act is different as is its scope. Section 2 of the Act says it is information about an identifiable individual that would generally only be known to the person themselves, their family and friends, or it is information held by a public body on the understanding it would be treated as confidential.

The Act states that the views or opinions of a person about an individual are classed as personal information. It also includes information regarding their educational, medical, psychiatric or psychological history, their financial affairs, employment or employment history, criminal history or information relating to their age, religion, sexual orientation or marital status. It also includes a person's entitlements under the Social Welfare Act, tax assessments, property as well as the view or opinions of another person about the individual.

However, what is not classed as personal information is what an employee of a public body does, writes or records as part of their job. In the case of a contractor, the Act says the information relating to the terms of the contract as well as anything they write or record in the course of the that contract are not classed as personal information.

There are several important issues to remember when considering using either piece of legislation. First, under the Data Protection Acts personal information can only relate to a person who is still alive, while under FOI it can relate to people who are deceased. Second, Data Protection covers all organisations including, for example, the Garda Siochána and the GAA, while FOI is only applicable to specific bodies, and, third, under FOI you can seek information about a specific individual (other than yourself) which can't be done under Data Protection.

Another important difference is that when making a request for personal information under the Data Protection Acts a requestor does not have to specify that the request is being made under this piece of legislation. It is assumed that the data controller is aware of their obligations to assist and answer such requests. In comparison, an application under the Freedom of Information Act must specify that it is being made under this piece of legislation.

Under the Data Protection Acts, there is no onus on the organisation to issue an acknowledgement that they have received the request, while under FOI such an acknowledgement should be issued within ten working days. Under the FOI Act, a full response should be given within 20 working days while under the Data Protection Acts, the decision maker (or data controller as they're generally called) has up to 40 days to gather the information and decide whether it should be released or not. The Data Protection Acts also expressly forbid amending information about a person after a request has been made but before the information is released unless it was going to be amended anyway.

The appeals processes between the two pieces of legislation are slightly different, but the key difference is that while FOI is designed to open up the State to public scrutiny, the Data Protection Acts are mainly aimed at protecting the individual's rights to privacy and preventing misuse of personal data by others.

How the data is collected by the organisation and stored are important in that they must receive the information by legitimate means, and the method of storage must be secure enough to prevent unauthorised access.

Requests for personal information covers records of all types including paper files, computers, discs or even closed circuit television systems (for example, security cameras).

Under both pieces of legislation there is a presumption that people can and should have access to information about themselves. While releasing personal information about others is prohibited under the Data Protection Act (with some exceptions), it is not totally exempt under the Freedom of Information Act, although it only happens in exceptional circumstances.

When you wish to make an application for personal information the first key element to establish is whether the information relates to you alone or could involve others. If it is information which involves others, or if it is even exclusively about others, then the best option is to use the Freedom of Information Act – provided the public body which holds the information is subject to FOI.

If it is information about yourself, then the Data Protection Act provides good scope to access the records you wish. However, as long as the request relates to you there is absolutely nothing to prevent you from using either piece of legislation.

It is important to repeat that the Freedom of Information Act is limited to specific bodies whereas the Data Protection Act is not limited – it applies to any organisation or company. That covers a vast array of State, semi-state, private and voluntary sector organisations such as your employer, your bank or sports club to give some examples.

When a request is made to a public body which is subject to FOI, the request must also be considered under the Data Protection Acts by the deciding officer. In effect, this means that when a request is made, either under FOI or the Data Protection Acts, by a person seeking their own personal information the deciding officer must consider both Acts irregardless of which Act the request was actually submitted under. To ensure this actually happens, a request could be submitted to a body subject to both Acts along the lines of:

> 'I wish to make an application to . . . for a copy of all records which relate to me. This application is being made under both the Freedom of Information Acts and the Data Protection Acts.'

This ensures that if, for example, a deciding officer rules that an application for personal information made under the Freedom of Information Act should be refused in part or in full, they must then consider the request under the Data Protection Act to see if the information can be released under that Act. If the decision is still to refuse then the letter stating this should inform the applicant of their rights to appeal.

The Acts do place some obligations on the requestors too. It is a common requirement under both pieces of legislation that the requestor submits enough information to identify themselves to the satisfaction of the official dealing with their request. It is also essential to identify the actual records being sought or the general type of information being requested.

Seeking personal information is one of the areas under FOI that does not need to be accompanied by a €15.00 payment to make the applications. Nor is there a fee payable for an internal appeal or for an appeal to the Information Commissioner. Likewise, there is no fee payable to an organisation when submitting a request under the Data Protection Acts. However, there may be charges for copying records held by the organisation which would have to be paid before they would be released.

Both FOI and the Data Protection Acts have sent down rigorous demands before personal information relating to others can be released. While both pieces of legislation allow for the personal information sought to be released if that other person agrees, under FOI personal information can also be released if the public interest is stronger than the individual's right to privacy. Proving this is not an easy task. A requestor must be able to prove to the satisfaction of the Information Commissioner that this case is exceptional and that it is right and proper that the information is released.

While the request was successful under FOI it would have failed if it had been sought under the Data Protection Acts. On the other hand, if you're just trying to find out information about a neighbour or friend or business partner then neither Act is likely to produce results for you. The bar for proving the public interest test regarding personal information is set pretty high and is not easily achieved.

The question of what is public interest in personal issues was at the heart of a long and expensive court case which concluded in July 2011 in the Supreme Court for which the taxpayer had to pick up the costs. Unfortunately, the Court, by majority decision, reduced the scope and power of the public interest in seeking information about a person.

In 2004 an elderly man sought details of his birth mother from the Rotunda Hospital. He was born in 1922 so the chances his mother was actually alive when the request was made were remote. The hospital released most information it had, but refused to release the age of the woman when her son was born. The man – who was making the request through his granddaughter – appealed that decision internally but was refused.

It then went to the Information Commissioner who said the age of the woman should be given on the grounds of the public interest to the individual concerned. The hospital appealed that to the High Court which rejected their case and instead agreed with the Commissioner that the age should be released to her son. The hospital, not satisfied with that, took the case to the Supreme Court where it won on a majority decision. The age of the woman was not to be released.

In the meantime, her son who had actually sought the information had died and the taxpayer had to pay tens – possibly hundreds – of thousands of euro in legal fees for the hospital and the Information Commissioner.

The hospital had already released information and the elderly man just wanted to know how old his mother was when she gave birth to him. That they refused to do and, ultimately, legally they were correct in their interpretation of the law.

In giving the majority judgement, Judge Nial Fennelly rather worryingly said that it was difficult to avoid the feeling that 'none of this great legislation would have taken place if it had not been for the Freedom of Information Acts' and this information could have been released. He suggested that a practical solution could possibly have been found if FOI had not been invoked, but once it was everyone was constrained by it.

However, the issue of real concern are the implications for releasing personal records under the public interest clause. The Supreme Court judge said he did not believe the section which provides for a public interest 'applies in a case where the reason for seeking access to the records is exclusively private'. It seems, in this judgement, that an individual cannot claim there is a public interest in them receiving information about another person, even if it is a member of their own family. For the public interest clause to succeed, the information must be sought on behalf of the public at large, such as through the media.

And while this decision has made it more difficult to obtain information about another person under FOI, it remains almost impossible under the Data Protection Acts. There is, for example, no 'public interest' element to this legislation and remember that the whole thrust of Data Protection is designed to protect, not release, personal information.

However, the Act does allow a data controller to release opinions written about the requestor without the consent of the author. This could take the form of letters of reference, for example. There are also provisions under both FOI and the Data Protection Acts for a data controller or deciding officer to release information but to withhold certain elements that would identify a person other than the requestor, such as a name or address or staff number.

There will always be instances where the requestor is not satisfied with the answers or information given to them and in that case the option to appeal comes into play. Under the Data Protection Acts, there is no internal appeal and the matter goes straight to the Data Protection Commissioner for a review and decision. Either the requestor or the body involved can appeal a Commissioner's decision to the Circuit Court and from there, on a point of law only, to the High and Supreme Courts.

One of the main reasons people make requests for personal information is to seek medical information about themselves. Again, while there is a presumption under both pieces of legislation that people are entitled to records relating to themselves, there are provisions in both Acts to limit this where the deciding officer believes it would not be in the best interests of the requestor to get that information. For example, it could relate to records surrounding issues of mental health or records of social workers.

Under the Freedom of Information Act, if a deciding officer comes to the conclusion that to release the records sought could be prejudicial to the requestor's physical or mental health, or emotional well-being, they can refuse the request. However, the Act does contain the option that the records could instead be released to a health professional (like a doctor or psychiatrist) chosen by the requestor. That person would then discuss the information directly with the requestor.

There's a similar provision under the Data Protection Acts where information should be withheld if giving it to the requestor would be likely to cause serious harm to the physical or mental health of the person who sought their own information. There is an option here too to consult with a health care professional.

There is a specific power under the Freedom of Information Act to allow parents or guardians to access information about their children or about a person with a physical or mental incapacity for whom they are responsible. The key factor here is proving to the satisfaction of the deciding officer that releasing the information is in the best interests of the individual child or person with disability. Whether it would be in the best interests of the parent or guardian is largely irrelevant.

However, there is no such entitlement under the Data Protection Acts. Disclosure is allowed to someone acting on behalf of a person but decisions on whether to release information is at the discretion of the data controller who decides the issues on a case by case basis.

As the Freedom of Information Act has a wide remit in that people can request information about any particular topic, there are also numerous exemptions aimed at preventing the release of data if it would cause harm or even just inconvenience for the State. Under the Data Protection Acts, there are also a wide range of exemptions although they are more limited than under FOI. These will be explored more fully over the coming pages.

Below is an overview of the main sections of the Data Protections Act 1988 and 2003.

Section 1: Interpretation and Application of the Act

This sets out the provisions of the Act and defines titles like 'data controller', 'disclosure' and 'direct marketing', for example. It defines 'personal data' as data relating to a living individual who is or can be identified either from the data itself or from the data in conjunction with other information that is in, or is likely to come into, the possession of the data controller.

Processing of data means the performance of any operation or task on the information such as: (a) obtaining, recording or keeping the information; (b) collecting, organising, storing, altering or adapting the information; (c) retrieving, consulting or using the information; (d) disclosing the information by transmitting, disseminating or making available; and (e) aligning, combining, blocking, erasing or destroying the information.

Sensitive personal data is defined as important information relating to the racial or ethnic origin, political opinions, religious or philosophical beliefs of the person, whether they are a member of a trade union, their physical or mental health or sexual life, the commission or alleged commission of an offence by the person or any proceedings against the person in a court.

This Section also states that the legislation apples to an individual who normally lives here, a body incorporated under Irish law, a partnership or unincorporated association and a legal entity (for example, company or business) who maintains an office, branch or agency in Ireland through which they carry on business here.

However, it does not apply to data kept 'solely for the purpose of historical research' or archives or departmental records within the meaning of the National Archives Act, that is, old records.

This Section also states that the Act does not apply to:

o   Personal information that in the opinion of the Minister for Defence is or was kept for the purpose of safeguarding the security of the state

o   Personal information that the data controller is required by law to make available to the public

o   Personal information kept by an individual and which relate to the management of their own personal or family affairs or data kept by an individual for recreational purposes.

Section 2: Protection of Privacy of Individuals with Regard to Personal Data

This Section states that a data controller must ensure that the data under their control was obtained and processed fairly and that it is accurate, complete and up to date. It also says that the information can only have been obtained for specific reasons and cannot be used for any other purpose; the body can only hold information it needs and not retain excessive amounts of data about a person; and finally that the data cannot be held for longer than necessary.

If personal data is only being retained for the purpose of direct marketing, a person can write to the data controller saying that the information is not to be processed for that purpose. Within forty days the information must be deleted by the data controller.

The processing of personal information can only be done if the individual has given consent and it is necessary for the performance of a contract involving the individual; for legal reasons; to prevent injury or harm (personal or financial) to the individual; for the administration of justice; for the functioning of the State or public interest; or for the 'legitimate interests' pursued by the data controller or third parties, but not when it is unwarranted.

> *The HSE Mid West and a consultant ophthalmic were both found to be in breach of the Data Protection Act in relation to obtaining information. A Limerick man suffered an eye injury in an incident and was attending a consultant doctor in his local hospital. Another consultant based in the same hospital but acting on behalf of an insurance company, sought and was given a copy of the man's medical file. The man complained to the Data Protection Commissioner and he upheld the complaint.*

This shows that personal information – particularly sensitive information should not be passed onto anyone without the consent of the person involved or unless it meets one of the criteria laid down in the Act.

This Section also acknowledges the harm that can come from unauthorised access or use of personal information and places the onus on the data controller to ensure that everyone who works for the organisation is aware of their obligations under the Data Protection Acts and that there is adequate security measures to protect the data.

Section 3: The Right to Establish Existence of Personal Data

This Section gives people a right to know if an organisation holds information about them. Anyone can make an application to any organisation and ask if it holds information about them. Under this Section, the data controller must respond within 21 days either confirming whether or not they have information about the requestor. If the organisation does have information they must tell the requestor what the information is and why they have it.

Section 4: Right of Access

This is the crucial section within the Data Protection Acts as it sets out the rights for people to access the actual information held by bodies about them. Following a request for information, a data controller must inform the person of the categories of data being held by them or on their behalf.

The person is also entitled under Section 4 to know the purposes for which the information is held, who the information may be disclosed to, and where the information came from (unless it is contrary to the public interest according to the Act but, as in FOI, there is no definition of public interest). The Section also states that the person to whom the information is being released should be given it in clear and understandable language, that is, not technical.gobbledegook.

If the information is important enough to have a significant impact on the person but it is processed only by automatic means, such as a computer programme, then the person is entitled – free of charge – to have the logic of the system explained to them, again in clear and understandable language.

Fees can also be imposed as set out by the Data Protection Commissioner, but the fees must be returned if the data held by an organisation has to be amended or deleted following release to the person involved.

Subsection (2) says that if there are separate pieces of data kept for various purposes by an organisation, they must treat a single request as a request for access to all information held.

Subsection (3) states that a person must give enough information to satisfy the data controller that they are who they say they are (to prevent information being given out to impostors).

Subsection (4) is important as it sets out the grounds under which information about a person other than the requestor can be released. For example, this could arise if someone sought access to their personnel file but that file contained comments or letters from another person about them.

The first part of the subsections states that an organisation is not obliged to disclose data to a person about another individual unless that individual has agreed to have the information released. However, if it is possible to keep that person's identity a secret by removing parts of the data (a name and address, for example) then the organisation is obliged to release this information with those elements removed. There is no such obligation under FOI.

Subsection (4A)(a) however goes on to say that if the information consists of an expression of opinion about the requestor, then that can be released without having to inform or get the permission of the author. There are exceptions here too, such as if the information is held on behalf of a person in charge of a place of detention (for example, a prison) or if the expression was 'given in confidence on the understanding that it could be treated as confidential'.

This last bit is significant. Firstly, it states that the information given on the understanding it 'could' be treated as confidential – not would, which is a much lower threshold – can be withheld. There is a significant divergence here with the Freedom of Information Act as the Information Commissioner has ruled on several occasions that, for example, letters of opinion about a person and should be released to the individual concerned even though the author was told the information would be treated as confidential.

> *Following an unsuccessful interview for a position, a man sought access to reference letters provided by his previous employers under the Freedom of Information Act. The Department refused saying the information had been provided in confidence. However, the Information Commissioner ruled that the requestor should be given access to the letters as they involved personal information relating to him. The Department, she ruled, could not give a guarantee that such information would always be kept confidential.*

Exam information too is also subject to Data Protection Acts. Examinations are not just the State exams, such as the Junior or Leaving Certificate, but are far broader under the definition in this Act. They are 'any process of determining the knowledge, intelligence, skill or ability of a person by reference to his performance in any test, work or activity'. This could the results of aptitude tests, written tests and interview notes.

Subsection (10) allows for data controllers to refuse to deal with repeated requests from individuals. It states that if the controller has previously complied with a request, then they are not obliged to comply with an identical or similar one from the same individual unless a reasonable interval has elapsed. This is similar to the provision in FOI to deal with 'frivolous and vexatious requests'.

Section 5: Restrictions to the Right of Access

Under subsection (1)(a) the Act does not apply to personal information which is kept for the purpose of 'preventing, detecting or investigating offences, apprehending or prosecuting offenders or assessing or collecting any tax, duty or other monies owed to the State, local authority or health board'.

Obviously it would be nonsensical if the gardaí or Revenue Commissioners had to release to a person they were investigating all the information they have about them. It would make law enforcement difficult to say the least, as it would, for example, allow criminals access to witness statements at a very early stage of an investigation.

However, to claim that records are exempt under this, the organisation has to be able to prove that allowing access would prejudice an investigation. If no harm could be done to such a probe, then the organisation has to release the information about a person when requested to do so.

Subsection (c) is aimed at preventing the release of personal information which would put at risk the security or the maintenance of good order in a prison or other place of detention.

Subsection (d) is a bit of a catch-all in that it states that any records kept for a function specified by the Minister for Justice to protect the public from financial loss are exempt. The next subsection exempts the release of records which would be 'contrary to the interests of protecting the international relations of the State'.

Subsection (f) covers records relating to the estimating of liability of an organisation on foot of a claim for compensation, for example from an insurance company, but again only when release would be prejudicial to the interests of the organisation.

Other subsections relate to data which is covered by legal privilege, information held by the Data Protection Commissioner and Information Commissioner as part of their work and statistical records where the identity of individuals are not released such as census data.

Section 6: Right of Rectification or Erasure

If the information held by an organisation is inaccurate, out of date or being held for a purpose not agreed to, then a person can under this section demand that the information be amended or deleted. However, there are certain exemptions, most notably to information processing by political parties, election candidates or holders of political offices during the course of election activities.

In general, the organisation must respond within 20 days of receiving the notification saying they will comply with the request to change or delete the information. The actions must be carried out within a further 20 day time period.

If the change to the information held is significant, and the original information has been passed on to another body within the previous twelve months of the amendment or deletion, then the organisation has to inform that other body of the changes.

However, if the organisation decides that the request to amend or alter is unjustified they must write to the person who was seeking the changes and state why they will not be complying.

If an appeal is made to the Data Protection Commissioner and he agrees that an organisation should comply with a request to amend or delete information, then under Section 6 he has the power to force the organisation to make the changes.

Under the same section it is also illegal for an organisation to rely purely on automatic systems (such as computer programmes) to make decisions which have serious consequences for the individual, such as creditworthiness, reliability, conduct and so on. There must be human input into such crucial decisions by an organisation although decisions which will not have a serious consequence, such as letters seeking business, can be fully automated.

Section 8: Disclosure of Personal Data in Certain Cases

This Section sets out the areas where the restrictions to the Act do not apply. These are if the data:

o   Is necessary for the security of the State as declared by a Garda Chief Superintendent or Colonel in the Defence Forces

o   Is necessary for the prevention, detection, investigation or prosecution of offenders or collection of taxes or duties

o   Is necessary for the protection of international relations of the State

o   Is necessary to prevent injury or damage to a person or property

o   Is required by law or by court order

o   Is necessary for legal advice of is part of a legal action

o   Is made at the request or with the consent of the person to whom the data relates.

There have been a number of cases involving workplace accidents where complaints against employers ended up before the Data Protection Commissioner.

Following an accident in her workplace, a woman sought a copy of all information held by her employers, Dairygold Co-Op. Although they failed to inform her within the 40 day period, the Co-Op eventually supplied some records to her. But not all. An internal accident report and an engineer's report were among those not released to the requestor. Dairygold claimed that both were prepared in case of a personal injuries claim and therefore had legal privilege so they didn't have to be released. The Data Protection Commissioner had to force the company to release the accident report. Hav-

> *ing viewed that and the engineer's report, the Commissioner pointed out that legal privilege was limited to correspondence between a client and their legal adviser. These documents were nothing of the sort and he ordered they be released to the woman.*

Section 10: Enforcement of Data Protection

This section sets out how the Data Protection Commissioner should set about their work. Following a complaint to the Commissioner they can investigate if there has been a breach of the Acts unless, according to subsection (b)(i), the Commissioner is of the opinion that it is frivolous or vexatious. The aim is always to find an amicable settlement, but if this is not possible then to issue a determination or decision on a case. Anyone who is unhappy with this decision has 21 days from the date it is issued to appeal to the Circuit Court.

If there is no appeal and the decision is in favour of the appellant, then the organisation has 21 days to make the changes or deletions ordered by the Commissioner. However, under this section the Commissioner also has the power to order changes or deletions within seven days if he decides that the enforcement notice should be complied with urgently.

Section 11: Restriction on Transfer of Personal Data Outside the State

As its title suggests, this section imposes limits on the information that can be sent to data controllers outside Ireland, the EU and the European Economic Area. It can only happen if the country where the data controller is to be based has 'an adequate level of protection' for this information and the rights of the individual although there are exemptions. These include for the fulfilling of contracts or legal requirements.

Section 21: Unauthorised Disclosure

Personal information held by a data controller cannot be released by them or by their employee or agent unless prior approval has been given by the data controller on behalf of the individual whose information is involved. Anyone who knowingly contravenes this is guilty of an offence.

Section 22: Disclosures of Personal Data Obtained Without Authority

Anyone who obtains personal information without the authority of the data controller and discloses that to another person is guilty of an offence under this section. There is also an important exemption here for personal information which is used for journalistic, artistic or literary purposes. Section 22 states that personal information processed for any of those reasons is exempt from compliance with any provision of the Act. However, this exemption only applies if:

o   The processing of the information is undertaken solely with a view to the publication of any journalist, literary or artistic material

o   The data controller reasonably believes there is a special importance of the public interest in freedom of expression that such publication of personal information is in the public interest (ie a 'whistleblower')

o   The data controller reasonably believes that compliance would be incompatible with journalistic, artistic or literary purposes.

Section 26: Appeals to the Courts

This section sets the process for appeals against decisions by the Data Protection Commissioner. In the first instance they must be heard in the Circuit Court, unlike decisions of the Information Commissioner in FOI cases which must be heard in the High Court.

Section 31: Penalties

Persons or organisations convicted of breaches of the Act can be fined up to €3,000, while for more serious breaches convictions on indictment can carry fines of up to €100,000.

So how do you actually go about requesting personal information from an organisation? You simply write to them! It can either be by email or ordinary post and should be addressed to the Data Protection Officer. In the letter or email you will need to give enough details about yourself so the organisation can identify you. This could be an account number or address or membership details. You should also be clear about what information you are looking for from the organisation. If you are not sure then you should ask for a copy of all the data they hold about you.

Although you do not have to mention the Data Protection Acts it is probably best that you do. You may have to pay a small fee to access the information. Your letter or email should be along the lines of:

'For the attention of the Data Protection Officer

Under the Data Protection Acts 1988 and 2003 I would like a copy of all the information you hold about me, how it was obtained and why it is being retained.

To help identify this data I include my address / former address / account number / date of birth.

I can be contacted via return e-mail or by post at the following address....

I look forward to hearing from you,

Regards,

[name]'

Do not be surprised if the organisation comes back and seeks additional information to ensure that you are who you say you are. If they released personal information to an imposter they would be in serious trouble.

If the organisation comes back and says they have no information about you then you can either rest assured or if you do not believe them then you can appeal to the Data Protection Commissioner.

If you hear nothing back from the organisation then contact them again and remind them of the original request. Inform them that this is an important matter for you and if they fail to engage with you the only alternative will be to bring the matter to the attention of the Data Protection Commissioner. If they still do not respond then the only option is to lodge that appeal.

If the organisation comes back and says yes we do have information about you and here it is, then it is up to you to check that it is accurate and that it was obtained fairly and is being retained for an agreed purpose. If not, contact the organisation, point out the problems and ask them to rectify them. If they do not do it within 40 days or if they refuse then the only option is to appeal to the Data Protection Commissioner.

Appeals again are a relatively straightforward and simple process. You can write or send an email to the Commissioner outlining your reasons for the appeal and why you think the organisation has not handled your request properly. This process is free of charge. In your letter or email you should clearly identify the organisation you made the request to and the person you have been dealing with. Describe in reasonable detail your concerns and how you tried to resolve them with the organisation and include their responses. It is a good idea too to include copies of any letters or emails between you and the organisation. All these will help the Commissioner get a quick grasp of the case at an early stage.

The Commissioner's office will try to resolve the issue informally between you and the organisation but if that fails the Commissioner will make a formal decision on whether your rights have been breached. If the Commissioner upholds your complaint he can force the organisation to comply with his ruling. If the Commissioner does not agree and rejects your appeal, then the only option is to appeal that decision to the Circuit Court.

There have been several interesting cases where the Commissioner upheld appeals by individuals against the State or media.

In July 2005, the Commissioner received a complaint from an individual who had requested a copy of all personal information held by the Garda Siochána. Some was released following the initial request but after the person sought a wider search, the gardai informed him that they had found more information in an archive. Over the coming months some of that information was released to the person. However, he lodged an appeal to the Commissioner over the fact that not all the data was being released to him.

During the investigation, staff from the Commissioner's office inspected all the personal data and there followed the release of more information. Overall, it took twelve months to resolve the case when the Act says it should be done within 40 days. The Commissioner was critical of the garda handling of this request, and in his decision noted that the case highlighted the fact that no data controller can consider themselves not bound by the Act.

> *In 2005, the Commissioner ruled that two newspapers, the Sunday World and the Irish edition of the News of the World had breached the Data Protection Acts by publishing information about celebrities. In the case of the News of the World, the complainant argued that a picture of her shopping with a child breached her right to privacy and it outweighed any purported journalistic or public interest.*
>
> *The newspaper argued that there was a journalistic and public interest in the picture and story, but the Commissioner disagreed. He cited a case from the European Court of Human Rights involving Princess Caroline of Monaco, which ruled that everyone is entitled to a legitimate expectation of protection for and respect of their private lives. In his ruling, the Commissioner pointed out that the media is subject to the Acts.*

The first question to be considered in cases relating to the media is whether there is a journalistic or public interest in publishing the information. If there is, then the other provisions of the Act are set aside. If there is not, then the Commissioner has warned that the media must have regard for their obligations under the Acts.

Of course, it is not just the Data Protection Acts that can be used to obtain personal information. The Freedom of Information Act is also a regularly used tool by people seeking to get information from State bodies about themselves.

Sections 17, 18 and 28 are the main ones used for this. Remember that while Data Protection Acts apply to all organisations, the Freedom of Information legislation only applies to certain specific bodies. And while DP is primarily of use to get information held about yourself FOI allows for applications seeking information about other people – but that will only be granted in occasional circumstances. For example, the chances of access the personal file of a neighbour who works in a Government Department are practically nil but getting certain information about senior officials in the public eye are somewhat better.

In several cases, the Commissioner has ruled that just because there is an FOI Act, that 'does not affect existing understandings that information about an individual of an essentially private character be treated as confidential'. Personal information is, generally speaking, information of a private nature.

Section 17 of the FOI Act is aimed at allowing people correct information held by a public body which is 'incomplete, incorrect or misleading'. Obviously you will need to have gotten the information from the organisation in the first place to see that it is incomplete, incorrect or misleading. If it is and you wish to have it corrected, you will have to provide sufficient information to the deciding officer to persuade them that what they have already is wrong and needs to be changed or updated. The deciding officer has four weeks to examine the information and conclude whether the changes requested are appropriate.

If the officer decides to reject the application, then they must still attach your request for change to the original document and inform you of your rights to appeal the decision. At first that is by way of an internal appeal within the organisation. Again you will need to set out your argument for the change you want. If that is rejected then you can appeal the matter to the Information Commissioner.

A deciding officer does not have to accept a request for change if that change is defamatory or unnecessarily voluminous.

If the change is accepted, the organisation 'shall take all reasonable steps' to notify other organisations or individuals who have had access to your information with the previous year that a change has been made. There are broadly similar requirements under the Data Protection Acts.

There's considerable case history involving Section 17 appeals to the Information Commissioner.

> *An applicant sought to have two records removed from her personal file which contained negative assessments of her performance. The then Eastern Health Board refused and that decision was upheld on appeal to the Commissioner, who ruled that simply holding a contrary opinion – without back-up evidence – was insufficient grounds for overturning the original decision.*

There have also been several cases where individuals sought to have points awarded in exams or in interviews to be re-examined via Section 17. The approach of the Commissioner is that she would be slow to change such decisions in the absence of strong evidence to back up the applicants claim. The Commissioner also accepted there is a degree of judgement and subjectivity in the decisions of any interview board which would make overturning such decisions extremely difficult. Section 18 contains the right of a person to information regarding actions or decisions of public bodies which affect them. It is closely linked to Section 17 and it allows for people personally affected by a decision to be given information about how that decision came to be made. To make an application under Section 18, a person must have 'a material interest in a matter . . . to be entitled to a statement of reasons'. This statement will include the reasons for the action or decision by the public body and 'any findings of any material issues of fact'.

However, Section 18 does not mean a requestor can get information which is included in an exempt record (for example, Government discussions), decisions of the Civil Service Commissioners, Local Appointment Commissioners regarding job selection, if releasing the record would be likely to prejudice the effectiveness of the selection process.

Section 18 is often used by people questioning social welfare and health-related issues, for example, or querying why they did not get a particular job, promotion or financial benefit such as a bonus.

The role of the Information Commissioner is not to re-examine the actual decision of the public body but instead to see if the organisation complied with Section 18 by providing a clearly understood statement, explaining how the body reached the decision it did. The Commissioner has stated in several decisions that it does not have to contain 'detailed clarification of all issues identified by a requester as relevant to a particular act or decision', that is, the body does not have to address and answer each issue raised by the requestor when giving their statement of reasons.

In an example cited in a decision, the Commissioner said that if someone failed to get a certain benefit because they did not receive full or correct information from a public official, then this would be revealed in a Section 18 statement. However, the Section does not mean the official has to explain why they failed to provide full or correct information – just that they did.

In summary, there are strengths and weaknesses to both and FOI processes. However, there is in both an underlying assumption that people are entitled to information about themselves, which is a good starting point!

10

An International Perspective

THERE ARE ESSENTIALLY TWO types of approach adopted by Governments to Freedom of Information around the world and they can be summarised as either the 'pull' or the 'push' approach. With the latter the State makes it easy to get information, usually by publishing large volumes online, while with the former the information has to be 'pulled' from the State.

The Irish approach is very much a 'pull', while others like Sweden, the US and increasingly the UK have the 'push' approach which sees considerable amount of data being made available to anyone and everyone.

Ireland was one of the first countries to adopt a Freedom of Information Act during the recent and rapid expansion of FOI around the world during the 1990s. Now almost all countries in Europe have FOI in some shape or form, although in Spain the idea is still just being discussed.

In most countries FOI is not limited to citizens or businesses located within its borders. Instead it is transnational in that requests can be made for information from people or companies based in other countries.

Many countries, particularly on Continental Europe, have what's known as the 'register system', where every record received by an organisation is entered on a register. Citizens can then in-

spect the register, see what records have been entered and ask to
see the record they're interested in.

'Wobbing' is also a word that FOI users into Continental Europe
will come across. It is a Dutch slang word created by journalists to
describe getting documents under Freedom of Information acts.

In this chapter we'll look at the FOI laws of three of the most
important countries and institutions relating to Ireland – the UK,
America and the European Union. We'll examine how to make requests and how to lodge appeals in each jurisdiction.

United Kingdom

The UK Freedom of Information Act, which covers England, Wales
and Northern Ireland, came into effect in 2005. There is a separate
and slightly more liberal Freedom of Information Act for Scotland.

The Acts are generally much more open and expansive than the
Irish version. For example, the UK Acts cover not only central government such as departments and agencies, but also local authorities and the health service down to the level of individual dentists,
doctors or opticians. Schools and colleges as well as universities are
covered, the police, the military, the regulators, publicly owned
companies as well as the Houses of Parliament, and the Northern
Ireland, Welsh and Scottish Assemblies.

This is a much wider range of bodies than are subject to FOI in
Ireland. For example, in the UK most State schools are subject to
the Act while in Ireland it's just some third level institutions. Dentists and doctors here are not under FOI nor is the military (as distinct from the Department of Defence) nor the gardaí or most publicly owned companies.

And there are many more differences: while only records created in Ireland after the Act came into force can usually be subject
to FOI, in the UK it is all records. Cabinet records are only accessi-

ble here after ten years but there is no such exemption in the UK. And while fees were introduced here to deter requests, in the UK the issue was examined and the decision made not to bring in fees simply because it would deter people from making requests.

Given that our civil service historically is so closely aligned to the British model it is inexcusable that our regime is far stricter than that which operates in the UK and Northern Ireland. It clearly shows that even in comparison to the British system, how secretive and restrictive FOI is in Ireland. And remember too that the Britain has adopted the European Directive on Accessing Information on the Environment – but without the 'mandatory' exemptions imposed in the Irish version. Even the secret services, MI5 and MI6 are subject to AIE but it has to be noted too that requests for information under AIE about the Monarchy, courts or tribunals in the UK are likely to be refused if they relate to anything other than administrative work.

Just like all other FOI Acts, the UK one gives people the right of access to records in whatever form they're held. It does not give access to information that is not written, typed or recorded somewhere. Bodies subject to FOI are not obliged under the British Acts to create records specifically for requests.

The history of FOI in the UK is even longer and more tortuous than it was here. Back in 1966, the Fulton Report recommended looking at ways to remove unnecessary secrecy. Six years later, the Local Government Act of 1972 allowed the public some access to the decision making process of local authorities.

In 1974 the Labour Party election manifesto pledged to bring in a Freedom of Information Act, but the following year after a visit to the US by Roy Jenkins does an about turn and the government decides it is not in favour of FOI. Despite this, the pledge to introduce it remained in every single Labour Party manifesto until 1997.

In December of that year the then Labour Government published a White Paper called 'Your Right to Know: The Government's Proposals for a Freedom of Information Act'. The plans were hailed as a very generous FOI Act but when the draft bill was published in May 1999 is was not as open.

The Bill was introduced in November 1999 and in its passage through the House of Commons there were several backbench revolts which led to improvements to the Act. The Bill eventually became law in December 2000, but it was a full five years later before it became operational.

'You idiot. You naive foolish irresponsible nincompoop.' These were the words of Tony Blair admonishing himself after introducing the Freedom of Information Act. Probably a fair assessment of how most leaders felt having introduced it, but compare it to comments made in 1996 – the year before he was elected Prime Minister - when he described FOI as 'change that is absolutely fundamental'.

The University College London's Constitutional Unit compared it to FOI regimes in Ireland, Australia, Canada and New Zealand 'and found it to be a highly restrictive bill by international standards'. That was before the Irish Act was 'amended' in 2003.

The British Act has many similarities to the Irish one, although it is generally less restrictive. It is worth noting that in Britain there is also a 'Central Clearing House' which is a centralised office where complex or sensitive FOI requests are discussed. Cynics have described it as more a method to keep an eye on controversial requests and give the government an opportunity to try to influence such requests or prepare responses when records are released. The Ministry of Justice, however, says the Central Clearing House is just there to provide advice, ensure consistency across central government departments and works to develop 'the boundaries of the legislation in accordance with government policy'.

To make a request it is, as always, crucial to decide what information or what type of data you're trying to find. Once you've that done it is best to examine the websites of the authorities likely to hold the records you're looking for to see if the information has already been released.

As part of a drive to make State information more accessible, the British Government launched a website, www.data.gov.uk, which contains a large array of information from a wide range of State bodies. For example, it lists all UK government spending over €25,000 on a department by department breakdown. It also lists senior civil servants and how much they earn as well as a list of all hospitality and gifts received by senior staff. It is possible, as a result, to look into a department and see how much they've spent on a particular area or issue. In Ireland some of that information would not be released while other data could only be accessed using FOI while.

These changes are likely to make the British Government the single largest producer of raw, open State information anywhere in the world. For example, in the health sector, it will allow people to compare clinical outcomes from doctors in England, look at prescription practices by GPs, complaints data and information on the clinical outcome of operations.

In the area of crime and justice, the plans will see sentencing information being made available online so people can see what sentences are being handed down in courts across the country, re-offending rates by criminals and the prisons they were in.

In the area of education, data will be published which will allow parents see how effective their locals schools are at teaching as well as school spending data.

These are just a few examples of the information that is being made available in the UK through the drive for more openness. In Ireland similar information is gathered in most of these areas which would allow such data to be published by the Government here if it so wished.

If you are seeking information from the UK it is possible that it has been released either on the organisation's own website or on data.gov.uk. However, depending on what you're looking for it may be that the information has not been published and remains within the organisation.

If that is the case, then you have to consider drafting a request to get it. The next step is to consider whether it is best to put the request in under FOI or the Environmental Information Regulations (EIR) as AIE is known in the UK.

If the information being sought is related to the environment then it is worth putting in the request under EIR. The legislation is identical to Ireland in terms of descriptions of what the environment is but the UK regulations do not have any mandatory exemptions that are specified in the Irish version. It is the case, however, that exclusions are almost certain in relation to requests about the monarchy and the legal system if trying to access information about a current criminal issue. The UK regulation also has one section which allows a minister to issue a certificate which exempts any record from release regardless of its content. This is not in the original EU Directive and therefore has questionable legal standing.

There are several ways to submit requests to UK bodies under FOI or EIR. They can be made directly to the organisation via e-mail, Twitter of Facebook, or a request can be sent via the excellent website, www.whatdotheyknow.com. Through this website you simply enter the name of the organisation you wish to send the request to, click on 'make a request', follow the simple checklist, write the request and press send. The one drawback to this website is that all the information including your request and the response you receive will be available for all to see on the website.

The alternative is to submit a request yourself which is also a very straightforward affair. When making a request to a UK government department or authority under FOI or EIR there are the usual few, common sense rules to apply. It is best practice to write an e-mail to the body and clearly state what you're looking for and your name. If you know exactly what documents you are seeking, you should state that in the request or you could ask first for a schedule or list of the records the body holds about the issue you are interested in. That could reveal that there are none, a few or a lot of records involved and would also open a dialogue with the FOI officer or the civil servant who is responsible for that particular section. Talking is often a better and quicker way to get information, and can certainly reduce the time wasted on unnecessary large scale 'trawls'. Of course, this also applies when making requests in other jurisdictions, including Ireland.

Although under the British regulations EIR requests can be made verbally, it is always best to send the request by e-mail. That removes any possibility of misunderstanding and also offers a clear communication path between you and the body. It is also possible to send FOI and EIR requests via social networking sites like Twitter. You should also state if the request is being made under FOI or EIR, and regardless which you choose send the request to the organisation's FOI officer or department.

Unlike Ireland where fees were introduced as a deterrent, there are no charges in the UK for making applications. The Labour Government of Gordon Brown did look at the issue but decided against it because fees would put up barriers to people requesting information and run contrary to the ideals of openness and transparency.

And just because you're sending a request from Ireland should make no difference under either FOI or EIR. Both pieces of legislation are 'applicant blind' in that it does not matter who asks for the information, where they are from or what they want the information for. Once you have sent off the e-mail with the request an ac-knowledgement should follow shortly afterwards.

Under the UK Acts an authority has twenty working days to re-spond to your request. They can also get an extension of another twenty days after informing you first. There is a surprisingly good response time from various authorities with, for example, the De-partment of Health responding to 99 per cent of requests within the twenty day limit while the Treasury responded to 95 per cent of requests within the limit. At the other end of the spectrum, the Ministry of Defence responded to just 60 per cent of requests within the timeframe. Under the Scottish FOI Act, there is no abil-ity to extend the time to answer a request.

Requests to schools can take up to sixty days to be answered if they're made close to or during holiday periods.

Most bodies in the UK which are subject to FOI have a link on their homepage where requests can be emailed. It is also possible to post a request to the FOI officer in the particular organisation once you know where their headquarters are.

Again, you should be as specific as possible when making the request. If you are not sure if the information is held by one or more particular bodies, you can send an FOI request to them all but be sure to mention that you list the organisations you've sent it to. It makes it easier if they all know they've received a similar or identical request so they know straight away who has been asked to supply the information.

Just like in Ireland it is a fairly common practice for the FOI of-ficers dealing with requests to get in touch to try to clarify some or all aspects of the request if it is vague or too broad.

While requests are free of charge, fees can be imposed for search, retrieval and copying of records. If the organisation esti-mates that the fees will amount to £600 for a Government depart-ment or £450 for all other bodies then they can refuse to meet your request on cost grounds. They may, on the other hand, offer to process the request as long as you're prepared to meet the full cost but the decision is up to the organisation to make.

And there's no point in trying to submit several smaller requests. If this is done and submitted within sixty days of each other the organisation is permitted to add up the costs of processing them altogether and then arriving at a total cost figure.

When you do get a final response from an authority it will have a covering letter stating the outcome of your request. It will inform you if records are being released or if some or all are being withheld and under what section of the Act that's being done under.

Records can be withheld for a variety of reasons under the UK and Scottish Acts. They can be broadly broken down into two areas, administrative and State. The administrative reasons include if the cost of meeting the request is over £600, if the authority has already provided you with similar information recently, if the request is 'vexatious' or if they do not hold the records you are seeking.

The State reasons are basically exemptions which can be split into two separate categories – ones which have no public interest clause, called 'absolute exemptions' and exemptions which do have public interest clause.

Absolute exemptions in the UK FOI Act are:

o Section 21, information already available;

o Section 23, information relating to or supplied by the security or intelligence services;

o Section 32, information only available in Court documents;

o Section 34, records covered by parliamentary privilege;

o Section 40, personal data;

o Section 41, if releasing information would breach confidentiality;

o Section 44, the disclosure of information which is not allowed by law.

The other sections where the FOI officer has discretion whether to release information having considered the public interest are:

o Section 22, information which is intended for publication;

o Section 24, information relating to national security;

o Section 26, information likely to harm the defence of the country;

o Section 27, information likely to harm international relations or information given in confidence from another government or international organisation;

o Section 28, information likely to harm administration;

o Section 29, information likely to harm economic interests;

o Section 30, information obtained during police investigations;

o Section 31, information likely to harm law enforcement or justice;

o Section 33, information likely to harm an auditing authority;

o Section 35, information relating to the formulation of government policy, ministerial communications, legal advise or records from a minister's private office;

o Section 36, information likely to harm the effective conduct of public business, prejudice collective responsibility or inhibit frank exchange of views;

o Section 38, information likely to cause risk to an individual;

o Section 42, information covered by legal professional privilege; and

o Section 43, information likely to harm trade secrets or commercial interests.

It's also important to note that, unlike in Ireland, requesters will not get a schedule of all the records which fall under the ambit of the request and then be told whether their information is being released or totally or partially withheld. In the UK requesters are just given a copy of the records being released and told if there are others and on what grounds those are being withheld. This is unfortunate as it makes appeals considerably more difficult to write as all you are told is that, for example, two records are being withheld under Section 24.

If you are not satisfied with the response from the State body the options are to give up or appeal. Unlike Ireland, appeals are free so it is worth appealing a decision to limit or refuse the information you receive. The letter you will have received from the agency should have details on it regarding your rights to appeal any aspect of their decision.

The appeals process is similar to the one in Ireland. The first step is an internal appeal in which you request the body to re-examine the decision. You can do this by e-mail or ordinary post. In making the appeal you should state it is being made under the Freedom of Information Act or the EIR and outline reasons why you believe the records should be released.

As with Irish appeals, the internal review is carried out by a more senior official within the organisation. They should look at the issue afresh. As also with Irish appeals it is well worth going through each section quoted for refusing to release a record and arguing why that is wrong and why the information should be released. This approach does take time but it does make the decision making process easier.

There are several sections of the UK and Scottish Acts which have a public interest clause and it is always worth highlighting that in any appeal, and remember, it is always up to the authority to justify their decision. There is no time limit within which to write the appeal but it is best done sooner rather than later while the body should give a decision within two to three weeks in simple appeals and six weeks in complex appeals.

If you are still not satisfied with the result of the internal appeal, then you can lodge an appeal with the Information Commissioner. In this appeal you should enclose copies of all correspondence with the body and, again, outline why you think the decisions to limit or refuse were wrong. As in Ireland, there is a presumption that the information should be released unless the body involved proves to the Commissioner's satisfaction that it is either subject to a mandatory exemption or that the public interest is best served by refusing to release.

Just like an appeal to the Information Commissioner in Ireland, it is worth taking the time to draft a detailed letter outlining the reasons why the records should be released in full. It is also a good idea to go through the list of previous decisions of the UK Commissioner (via their website) and find cases that back up your arguments. There is a simple search engine on the Commissioner's website which allows a search on a section-by-section basis.

Unlike the Irish system where the Commissioner is the last avenue of appeal unless someone is willing to start a High Court action, in the UK if people are still dissatisfied after the decision of the Information Commissioner they can bring an appeal to the Information Tribunal. This is part of a wider tribunal system in the UK which comprises several tribunals such as the Gambling Appeals Tribunal and the Family Health Services Appeal Authority, for example.

If you have the money you can retain legal counsel at this stage in the appeals process but it is not necessary. The First Tier Tribunal is chaired by a Tribunal judge and two non-legal members. You can opt for an oral appeal where you attend the hearing as does counsel from the Information Commissioner, or you can say you would prefer a paper-based appeal where the arguments are simply written out and considered by the panel. Usually, paper-based appeals are heard quicker but the final decision on whether there is a paper or oral hearing rests with the Tribunal itself. Each side usually pays their own legal costs.

This process takes time (or money) to prepare and should not be undertaken lightly. An appeal from here to the Upper Tier Tribunal can only be based on a point of law, and from there into the full legal system through the High Court. The success rate of overturning Commissioner's decisions is not high but it does happen.

It is also worth noting that even if the Commissioner decides to grant your appeal, that decision can be overturned by a Minister. Members of the Cabinet can veto any decision by the Commissioner or the Information Tribunal.

European Union

The power and influence of the European Union over our day-to-day lives has largely been ignored by most citizens, not just in Ireland but in most member countries. There continues to be a perception that Europe is 'over there' somewhere and what happens there has a relatively limited impact over here.

The labyrinthine structures of the European Union do not make it easy to understand and that, together with the disconnect between the EU and many of its citizens, has led to the EU 'FOI' legislation being almost totally ignored here. Also being ignored are plans by the EU to tighten up on this important piece of legislation.

Regulation 1049/2001 outlines the importance of openness which:

> '. . . enables citizens to participate more closely in the decision-making process and guarantees that the administration enjoys greater legitimacy and is more effective

and more accountable to the citizen in a democratic system. Openness contributes to strengthening the principles of democracy and respect for fundamental rights.'

However, despite the lofty ideals there are many obstacles to getting information from the European Parliament, European Council and the European Commission.

In fact, in several ways the EU regulation mirrors Ireland's FOI Act. There are many significant bodies outside the reach of citizen inquiry, there are significant issues regarding the curtailment of the regulation and problems with the bodies that are subject of the regulation.

Under 1049/2001 any person or organisation either inside or outside the EU can submit a request. The easiest way is to send the request via e-mail which can be submitted in any of the official European Union languages. English, French or German are probably the best languages to use for the request.

The regulation covers all documents drawn up, received and in the possession of the European Parliament, Council or Commission. Like all other FOI Acts, it only relates to records and does cover knowledge known by officials but not committed to record somewhere. The definition of document is one that covers 'any content whatever its medium (written on paper or stored in electronic form or as a sound, visual or audiovisual recording) concerning a matter relating to the policies, activities and decisions falling within the institution's sphere of responsibility'. Unsurprisingly, there are exemptions under the Regulation too. Generally, they cover the similar sort of areas which are restricted under the far from liberal Irish FOI Act.

A new website has been launched recently which will make it substantially easier to submit requests. Based on a similar website in the UK, www.asktheeu.org is run by groups promoting open access and the website allows people to submit requests online. The request is routed to the various parts of the EU and then a reply is sent back to the website. They pass it on to the requestor and publish it on their website. It will prove to be an invaluable tool to citizens interesting in obtaining information from the EU. The only drawback is that requests and the replies will be published on the website for all to see.

Article 4(1)(a) of 1049/2001 states that the Institution which receives the request 'shall' refuse if disclosure would undermine the protection of the public interest relating to security, defence and military matters, international relations, the financial or monetary or economic policy of the Community or an individual member state. There is no public interest clause in this exemption.

Article 4(1)(b) says that the exemptions also apply to the release of records which would undermine the privacy or an individual. Similarly, there is no public interest clause in this exemption.

Article 4(2) says the institution shall refuse to release a document if it would undermine the protection of the commercial interests of a person or business, court proceedings and legal advice or undermine inspections, investigations and audits – unless there is 'an overriding public interest in disclosure'.

Article 4(3) states that a document drawn up by an institution for internal use or received by them and which relates to an issue where a decision has not been taken 'shall be refused' if disclosure would 'seriously undermine the institution's decision making process' unless there is an overriding public interest. There has been much criticism of the overuse of this particular section by the EU to prevent documents being released.

Article 4(4) relates to records provided by an outside body. It states that an institution shall consult with them with a view to see whether an exemption should be applied unless it is evident that the document should or should not be released.

Article 4(5) says that if a Member State provides any document it cannot be released by the Institution without prior approval.

Despite all these restrictions, there is still plenty of scope to get useful information from the EU which could be of interest or benefit to many.

In making an application you should be as specific as possible and mention that the request for information is being made under Regulation 1049/2001, which sets out a process for the institution to follow. There are no charges for making a request under these regulations.

Once you've decided to seek information you'll face the first hurdle – where do you send the request. In 2009, the Madrid-based human rights organisation Access Info Europe carried out a detailed examination of the process to submit requests and found that many problems existed, especially surrounding the basic start point – where to send the request!

Their investigation was instigated by the leaking of an internal memo from the Directorate General for Trade, which advised staff on how to avoid putting certain information down on record and how to prevent the release of information as well. It suggested that staff create two documents, one which would contain just factual information and the second which would contain the real information such as an assessment or analysis of the issues. Of course, any requester would just be issued with the first record.

The best place to try to find where to send it is to literally rummage around the organisation's website looking for an email address. The link entitled 'contact us' is usually the best option. On some sites you have to fill in mandatory questions which would never be asked in a straightforward FOI request. If you have a problem locating where to send the e-mail remember that the European Parliament and the European Commission both have offices in Dublin who should be able to assist.

Once the body has received the e-mail or letter they have to issue an acknowledgement that they have received your request, make a decision and respond to you within fifteen working days. In complex cases, they are allowed to extend that by a further fifteen working days. If records are being released the organisation can only charge for copying the documents – they cannot charge for search and retrieval of the data concerned.

However, if you receive no response to your request it is deemed as a refusal and you can appeal. It's the same story if your request is partially or totally rejected. You have fifteen working days in which to write and send your appeal. Under EU regulations this appeal is called a 'confirmatory application' where you ask the institution to reconsider the original decision.

If this is rejected or you hear nothing back within the fifteen days then you have two choices. You can start court proceedings which are expensive and therefore an effective deterrent, while the other option is to appeal to the European Ombudsman. It's interesting to note that according to the 2010 annual report, the Ombudsman only received 2,667 appeals for the entire year out of an EU population of over 500 million people. One-third of all appeals related to the lack of transparency within the EU and the refusal to release information and documents. That is alarmingly high.

However, the key issue to remember with using 1049/2010 is that the process is relatively straightforward – once you know where to start and are determined enough to follow through. There is, of course, no guarantee of success but if no one asks no one will be told.

The EU also has plans, like the FF/PD government, to 'improve' this model of citizen's access to information. The proposals would largely have the same effect on the law as the 2003 review of the legislation did in Ireland, that is, change it dramatically for the worse. Following their review, Access Info Europe concluded that the Commission's plans which were first revealed in 2008 would:

> '. . . reduce the right of Europe's citizens to know about decision making, the exercise of power, legislative initiatives and the spending of public funds in Brussels. . . . The result is likely to be a greater distancing of citizens from Union institutions and a lowering of public trust.'

And to emphasise just how difficult the situation is many countries (including Ireland) refused to reveal to the group their views on the Commission's proposals. The Irish decision meant that only Brussels could tell Irish citizens what the Irish Government's view was on the issue!

Among the Commission's plans are some very restrictive measures. For example, when is a document not a document? That's a question that arises under the Commission's proposals. Under the current interpretation of the regulations a record is anything that is recorded in physical form, but under the Commission plan a record will only officially exist if it has been circulated within the institution or placed on the official register of documents.

Even the Commission itself has acknowledged that it has major failings with its register and that it is not even close to putting all records it receives or creates on the official register. The proposed changes therefore could lead to the bizarre situation were a record may be on an official's desk but because it is not entered on the register it does not 'exist' and cannot be released! The plans are being opposed by the European Parliament but there is no guarantee that the Commission's view will not win the day. The Parliament's view is that the scope of the regulations should actually be widened to encompass all EU organisations such as the European Central Bank, the European Courts of Justice and Europol, all of which are outside the scope of 1049/2001. The MEPs also want to develop easier to use mechanisms so more citizens can have access to more information.

USA

On July 4, 1966 a disgruntled President Lyndon Johnson signed the Freedom of Information Act into law in America. He did it without fanfare while on holiday at his Texas ranch, and he did it very reluctantly because he despised FOI and what it was setting out to do. 'The Justice Department tells me this goddamn bill will screw the Johnson Administration,' he said. He was not alone. There was strong opposition from almost all federal agencies to the Act.

Certain aspects of Freedom of Information seem to be mirrored in country after country, and it was the same in America. The Republicans had been disinterested in the Act while in government, but that changed during the Kennedy and Johnson administrations. Donald Rumsfeld, then a young Republican from Illinois, denounced Johnson for his 'continuing tendency toward managed news and suppression of pubic information that the people are entitled to have'. Within a decade, as White House Chief of Staff, Rumsfeld would lead President Ford's efforts to veto attempts to strengthen FOI.

When America enacted FOI in 1966, it became just the third country to do so after Sweden and Finland. Nowadays the federal and state agencies in the US process several million requests under FOI every year.

The mechanism for FOI requests to American agencies is pretty similar to the system in operation here and in most other countries. If you wish to find out information from an American Federal or State body, the first step is to establish what exactly you want. Once that is done, go to the organisation's website and search there to see if the information has already been released. As part of the American

FOIA there's a requirement to publish considerable amounts of data in their electronic 'reading rooms' so it is possible that what you're seeking has already been released. It's common to find documents or frequently requested information contained in such 'reading rooms'. The 'reading rooms' can be a valuable source of information as popular issues or commonly requested records can be located here. For example in the FBI 'reading room' there's everything from Saddam Hussein to the Roswell Incident to the Columbine High School massacre. 'Reading rooms' can be found on the agency's website, usually by following the FOIA link on the homepage.

Depending on what you're seeking it is worth taking time to check whether the information is there, but once you've satisfied yourself that it is not then it's time to consider sending in an FOI request. The request must mention that it is being made under the Freedom of Information Act, be made in writing via post or e-mail, and must contain enough information to allow the official clearly to work out what is being requested. It is important to be as clear as possible in making a request because, depending on the agency involved, your request could potentially involve a search of tens of thousands of records.

Clearly, you must also include return contact details in your request and as you're likely to be making it from Ireland it is probably best to make the original request via e-mail as it allows for prompt correspondence between you and the agency. Having drawn up the request the next challenge is figuring out who to send it to. All government departments and Federal agencies in America are subject to FOI. A good starting point is the Department of Justice's website which lists all bodies which are subject to FOIA. While there are many, many organisations which are under FOIA, there are others which are not. The office of the President and Vice President and their immediate staff are not, nor are the specific offices set up to advise them such as the National Security Council. However, it has become practice to release Presidential records between five and twelve years after they have left office.

There are a number of similarities with the Irish FOI including the exclusion of politician's records from the Act. Just like the information held by a TD or Senator is exempt, so too are records belonging to a member of Congress. Court records are not subject to the Act in either jurisdiction but in America they do not need to be as they are regarded as public information as a result of the Constitution and therefore accessible by the public.

Where a contractor doing work on behalf of a State body in Ireland is subject to FOI in relation to that work, the same does not apply in America. In the States, private companies are exempt even if they are fully funded by the taxpayer or if they are doing work on behalf of the State.

Once you have figured out which agency is most likely to have the information you want, it could be worthwhile contacting their FOIA office informally and asking if they records have been released already, or if they can be released without putting them and you through the formality of making a request. In my experience I've found American civil servants are far more open to giving out information so this approach may yield results.

If it does not then the next step is to send in the FOIA request. In all agencies there is an FOIA office and staff but in some larger organisations like Defence there are various sub-offices and regional offices which are all responsible for various parts of the service. If you can establish (maybe from the central FOIA office) which specific office would deal with your request then it can be sent directly to them. Failing that, send it to the organisation's head office.

Once it has been received the agency has twenty working days in which to respond, but very few requests are answered within that timeframe. Many agencies have adopted a two-speed approach to FOIA. If a request is for a small number of documents and they can be readily identified then it is likely that request will be responded to fairly quickly. Longer and more complex requests involving a large number of records are likely to be put into a longer and larger queue with similar requests.

Unusually, it is possible under the American FOI system to request an agency to speed up the processing of your request, but this can only be done in exceptional circumstances. To do this you must ask for it and outline why this is necessary. For reporters their requests can be expedited far easier if the information being sought relates to a matter of 'compelling concern'.

Agencies may charge 'reasonable' fees for the costs of searching, retrieving and copying of the records sought, but these can be waived if there is a public interest in revealing the information being sought.

There are four separate categories relating to costs within the American system. Those seeking the information for commercial use must pay the full cost of retrieval and copying; non-commercial requests from educational or scientific bodies pay no search fees and receive 100 pages of free copying (after that it costs); reporters pay no search fees and get 100 pages of copying free; while all other requests receive two hours of search time and copies of 100 pages free.

There is also an internal appeals mechanism in cases where the requester disputes the fees the body wishes to charge. Appeals can also be lodged if there is partial or total refusal or to release information, or if the agency has failed to meet the 20-day deadline, although because of the backlog of cases courts have been somewhat reluctant to act on the last element too quickly.

The appeal is a simple letter or e-mail to the agency's administrator and, like the Irish Act, if specific sections are cited for refusing or limiting the release of information they should be addressed in your appeal. You should also mention the issue of public interest and say that this interest is best served by releasing the information and show how that is the case.

If the appeal is ignored or refused the only option then is to take the matter to the court and file a case with the United States District Court. From Ireland that is pretty much impractical so it is often best to try and negotiate with the agency over the exempt records.

Overall, agencies are well practiced in FOI in the States and obtaining information, while slow, is often well worth the effort.

Appendix 1

Public Bodies Subject to the Freedom of Information Act

Government Departments

Department of Agriculture, Fisheries and Food

Department of Arts, Heritage and the Gaeltacht

Department of Children and Youth Affairs

Department of Communications, Energy and Natural Resources

Department of Defence

Department of Education and Skills

Department of Environment, Community and Local Government

Department of Finance

Department of Foreign Affairs and Trade

Department of Health

Department of Jobs, Enterprise and Innovation

Department of Public Expenditure and Reform

Department of Social Protection

Department of the Taoiseach

Department of Tourism, Culture and Sport

Department of Justice and Equality

State agencies and bodies subject to the Freedom of Information Act

Affordable Homes Partnership

An Bord Altranais

An Chomhairle um Oideachas Gaeltachta & Gaelscolaíochta

An Daingean Education Support Centre

Appeal Commissioners for the purposes of the Tax Acts,

Aquaculture Licensing Appeals Board

Army Pensions Board

Arts Council, The

Athlone Education Support Centre

Attorney General, Office of the

Blackrock Education Support Centre

An Bord Bia

Bord Iascaigh Mhara, An

Bord na gCon

Bord na Leabhar Gaeilge

An Bord Pleanála

BreastCheck The National Cancer Screening Service

Carlow County Enterprise Board

Carlow Education Support Centre

Carrick-on-Shannon Education Support Centre

Cavan County Enterprise Board

Cavan Education Support Centre

Censorship of Publications Board

Censorship of Publications Appeal Board

Central Statistics Office

Chester Beatty Library

Chief State Solicitor, Office of the

Children Acts Advisory Board

Chomhairle Leabharlanna, An

Citizens Information Board

Civil Defence Board

Clare County Enterprise Board

Clare Education Support Centre

Classification of Films Appeal Board

Chief Medical Officer of the Civil Service

Coimisiún Logainmneacha, An

Comhairle na Nimheanna (The Poisons Council)

Commission for Aviation Regulation

Commission for Energy Regulation

Commissioners of Charitable Donations and Bequests

Commission for Communications Regulation

Commission for Public Service Appointments, Office of the

Commission for Taxi Regulation

Companies Registration Office

Company Law Review Group

Competition Authority

Comptroller and Auditor General, Office of

Connemara & Árann Education Support Centre

Cork City Enterprise Board

Cork Education Support Centre

Cork North Enterprise Board

Courts Service

Crafts Council of Ireland

Criminal Injuries Compensation Tribunal

Crisis Pregancy Agency

Defence Forces

Dental Council

Dental Health Foundation

Digital Hub Development Agency

Director of Corporate Enforcement, Office of the

Director of Public Prosecutions, Office of the

Donegal County Enterprise Board

Donegal Education Centre

Drug Treatment Centre Board

Drumcondra Education Centre

Dublin City Enterprise Board

Dublin Docklands Development Authority

Dublin Institute for Advanced Studies

Dublin Transportation Office

Dublin West Education Support Centre

Dun Laoghaire Rathdown County Enterprise Board

Dundalk Education Support Centre

Enterprise Ireland

Environmental Protection Agency

Equality Authority

European Regional Development Fund

European Social Fund Financial Control Unit

Family Support Agency

FAS / SOLAS

Fingal County Enterprise Board

Fire Services Council

Food Safety Authority of Ireland

Forfás

Further Education & Training Awards Council

Fáilte Ireland

FÁS International Consulting Limited

Gaisce Gradam an Uachtarain

Galway City and County Enterprise Board

Galway Education Centre

Gort a Choirce Education Support Centre

Health Information and Quality Authority

Health Information and Quality Authority, The

Health Insurance Authority

Health Research Board

Heritage Council, The

Higher Education and Training Awards

Horse Racing Ireland

Houses of the Oireachtas Commission

Housing Finance Agency

Health and Safety Authority of Ireland

Irish Blood Transfusion Services Board, The

Industrial Development Agency

Information Commissioner, Office of the

Institute of Public Administration

Integrate Ireland Language and Training Awards

International Education Board of Ireland

Ireland - US Commission for Educational Exchange, Fulbright Commission

Irish Film Board

Irish Film Classification Office

Irish Human Rights Commission

Irish Manuscripts Commission

Irish Medicines Board

Irish Museum of Modern Art

Irish National Stud

Irish Research Council for Science, Engineering and Technology

Irish Research Council for the Humanities and Social Sciences

Irish Sports Council

Irish Water Safety Association

Kerry County Enterprise Board

Kildare County Enterprise Board

Kildare Education centre

Kilkenny County Enterprise Board

Kilkenny Education Support Centre

Labour Relations Commission

Laois County Enterprise Board

Laois Education Centre

Leargas The Exchange Bureau

Legal Aid Board

Leitrim Enterprise Board

Limerick City Enterprise Board

Limerick County Enterprise Board

Limerick Education Centre

Local Government Management Services Board

Local Government Computer Services Board

Longford Enterprise Board

Louth County Enterprise Board

Marine Institute

Mayo Enterprise Board

Mayo Education Centre

Meath Enterprise Board

Medical Bureau of Road Safety

Medical Council

Mental Health Commission

Mining Board

Monaghan Enterprise Board

Monaghan Education Centre

National Council for Curriculum and Assessment

National Advisory Committee on Drugs

National Archives

National Building Agency

National Cancer Registry, Ireland

National Centre for Guidance in Education

National Centre for Technology in Education

National College of Ireland

National Concert Hall

National Consumer Agency

National Council for Special Education

National Council for the Professional Development of Nursing and
Midwifery

National Disability Authority

National Drugs Strategy Team

National Economic and Social Council

National Education Welfare Board

National Gallery of Ireland

National Library of Ireland

National Milk Agency

National Museum of Ireland

National Qualifications Authority of Ireland

National Roads Authority

National Safety Council

National Social Work Qualifications Board

National Sports Campus Development Authority

National Standards Authority of Ireland

National Statistics Board

National Tourism Development Agency

National Treatment Purchase Fund

Navan Education Centre

Offaly County Enterprise Board

Office of Public Works

Office of the Pensions Ombudsman

Office of Tobacco Control

Ombudsman, Office of the

Ombudsman for Children, Office of the

Opticians Board

Ordinance Survey Ireland

Patents Office

Pensions Board

Performance Verification Group: Civil Service

Performance Verification Group: Education Sector

Performance Verification Group: Health Service

Performance Verification Group: Justice and Equality Sector

Performance Verification Group: Local Government

Pharmaceutical Society of Ireland

Pobal

Postgraduate Medical and Dental Board

Pre-Hospital Emergency Care Council

Probation Service

Public Appointments Service

Radiological Protection Institute of Ireland

Railway Procurement Agency

Registrar of Friendly Societies, Office of the

Registration of Titles Rules Committee

Registry of Deeds

Rent Tribunal

Revenue Commissioners, Office of the

Roscommon County Enterprise Board

Royal College of Surgeons in Ireland

Royal Irish Academy

Royal Irish Academy of Music

Science Foundation Ireland

Shannon Development

Skillnets.Ltd

Sligo County Enterprise Board

Sligo Education Support Centre

Social Welfare Appeals Office

Social Welfare Tribunal

SOLAS

South Cork Enterprise Board

South Dublin Enterprise Board

Standards in Public Office Commission

State Laboratory

Sustainable Energy Ireland

Tarbert Edcuation Support Centre

Teaching Council, The

Teagasc

The Marine Casualty Investigation Board

Thurles Education Support Centre

Tipperary North County Enterprise Board

Tipperary South County Enterprise Board

Tralee Education Support Centre

Tuam Education Support Centre

Údarás na Gaeltachta

Valuation Office Ireland

Valuation Tribunal

Veterinary Council of Ireland

Victim Support

Waterford City Enterprise Board

Waterford County Enterprise Board

Waterford Education Support Centre

West Cork Education Centre

West Cork Enterprise Board

Western Development Commission

Westmeath County Enterprise Board

Wexford Enterprise Board

Wexford Education Centre

Wicklow County Enterprise Board

City, County, Borough, Town Councils

Carlow County Council

Cavan County Council

Clare County Council

Cork City Council

Cork County Council

Donegal County Council

Dublin City Council

Dun Laoghaire/Rathdown County Council

Fingal County Council

Galway City Council

Galway County Council

Kerry County Council

Kildare County Council

Kilkenny County Council

Laois County Council

Leitrim County Council

Limerick City Council

Limerick County Council

Longford County Council

Louth County Council

Mayo County Council

Meath County Council

Monaghan County Council

North Tipperary County Council

Offaly County Council

Roscommon County Council

Sligo County Council

South Dublin County Council

South Tipperary County Council

Waterford City Council

Waterford County Council

Westmeath County Council

Wexford County Council

Wicklow County Council

Clonmel Borough Council

Drogheda Borough Council

Sligo Borough Council
Wexford Borough Council
Kilkenny Borough Council

Arklow Town Council
Athlone Town Council
Athy Town Council
Ballina Town Council
Ballinasloe Town Council
Birr Town Council
Bray Town Council
Buncrana Town Council
Bundoran Town Council
Carlow Town Council
Carrickmacross Town Council
Carrick-on-Suir Town Council
Cashel Town Council
Castlebar Town Council
Castleblaney Town Council
Cavan Town Council
Clonakilty Town Council
Clones Town Council
Cobh Town Council
Dundalk Town Council
Dungarvan Town Council
Ennis Town Council
Enniscorthy Town Council
Fermoy Town Council
Kells Town Council
Killarney Town Council
Kilrush Town Council
Kinsale Town Council

Letterkenny Town Council
Listowel Town Council
Longford Town Council
Macroom Town Council
Mallow Town Council
Midleton Town Council
Monaghan Town Council
Naas Town Council
Navan Town Council
Nenagh Town Council
New Ross Town Council
Skibbereen Town Council
Templemore Town Council
Thurles Town Council
Tipperary Town Council
Tralee Town Council
Trim Town Council
Tullamore Town Council
Westport Town Council
Wicklow Town Council
Youghal Town Council

Ardee Town Council
Bagenalstown Town Council
Balbriggan Town Council
Ballybay Town Council
Ballshannon Town Council
Bandon Town Council
Bantry Town Council
Belturbet Town Council
Boyle Town Council
Cootehill Town Council

Droichead Nua Town Council

Edenderry Town Council

Gorey Town Council

Granard Town Council

Greystones Town Council

Kilkee Town Council

Leixlip Town Council

Lismore Town Council

Loughrea Town Council

Muinebheag Town Council

Mountmellick Town Council

Mullingar Town Council

Passage West Town Council

Portlaoise Town Council

Shannon Town Council

Tramore Town Council

Tuam Town Council

Regional Authorities and Regional Assemblies

Border Regional Authority

Border, Midland and Western Regional Assembly

Dublin Regional Authority

Mid-East Regional Authority

Midland Regional Authority

Mid West Regional Authority

South-East Regional Authority

Southern & Eastern Regional Assembly

South West Regional Authority

West Regional Authority

The Health Service Executive

Health Service Executive

Dublin – Mid Leinster

Dublin – North East

HSE South

HSE West

Health Protection Surveillance Centre

Health Service Employers Agency

Voluntary Hospitals

Adelaide and Meath Hospital, incorporating the National Children's Hospital

Beaumont Hospital

Cappagh National Orthopaedic Hospital

Central Remedial Clinic

Children's University Hospital

City of Dublin Skin and Cancer Hospital

Coombe Women's Hospital

Dublin Dental Hospital

Incorporated Orthopaedic Hospital of Ireland

Leopardstown Park Hospital

Mater Misericordiae University Hospital

Mercy Hospital

National Maternity Hospital

National Rehabilitation Hospital

Our Lady's Hospice Harold's Cross Limited

Our Lady's Hospital for Sick Children

Rotunda Hospital

Royal Hospital

Royal Victoria Eye and Ear Hospital

South Infirmary - Victoria Hospital

St. Francis Hospice

St. James's Hospital

St. John's Hospital

St. Luke's Hospital

St. Mary's Hospital and Residential School

St. Michael's Hospital

St. Patrick's Hospital / Marymount Hospice

St. Vincent's Hospital

St. Vincent's University Hospital

Services for persons with intellectual disabilities

Brothers of Charity Services (Mid-West Region)

Brothers of Charity Services, Galway

Brothers of Charity Services, Roscommon

Brothers of Charity Services, Waterford

Brothers of Charity Southern Services

Camphill Communities

Cheeverstown House

COPE Foundation

Daughters of Charity of St Vincent de Paul

Ability West

Hospitaller Order of St. John of God Services

Irish Sisters of Charity

KARE

Peamount Hospital

Rosminian Services

Sisters of Charity of Jesus and Mary Services/Muiríosa Foundation

Sisters of Charity of Jesus and Mary, Monasterevin

Sisters of La Sagesse Services

Sisters of the Bon Savueur

Sisters of the Sacred Hearts of Jesus and Mary Services

St. Mary of the Angels
St. Michael's House
Stewart's Hospital Services Limited
Sunbeam House Services
Western Care Association

Services for persons with physical disabilities

Enable Ireland
Irish Wheelchair Association
Cheshire Ireland
Multiple Sclerosis Society of Ireland,
The National Council for the Blind of Ireland, The
DeafHear.ie

The broadcasting sector

Broadcasting Authority of Ireland
DTT Network Company
Radio Telefís Éireann
RTE Commercial Enterprises
RTE Music Limited
TG4 (Seirbhísí Theilifís Na Gaeilge Teoranta)

Third level sector

Athlone Institute of Technology
Church of Ireland College of Education
Coláiste Mhuire Marino
Cork Institute of Technology
Dublin City University
Dublin Institute of Technology
Dún Laoghaire Institute of Art, Design and Technology
Dundalk Institute of Technology

Froebel College of Education

Galway-Mayo Institute of Technology

Higher Education Authority

Institute of Technology, Blanchardstown

Institute of Technology, Carlow

Institute of Technology, Sligo

Institute of Technology, Tallaght

Institute of Technology, Tralee

Letterkenny Institute of Technology

Limerick Institute of Technology

Mary Immaculate College

Mater Dei Institute of Education

National College of Art & Design

National University of Ireland, Galway

National University of Ireland, Maynooth

St. Angela's College

St. Catherine's College of Education for Home Economics

St. Patrick's College

Tipperary Institute

Trinity College Dublin

University College Cork

University College Dublin

University of Limerick

Waterford Institute of Technology

National University of Ireland

Fisheries Boards

Inland Fisheries Ireland

Appendix 2

Useful Websites

Ireland

www.oic.gov.ie – The Office of the Information Commissioner who is charged with overseeing the implementation of Freedom of Information legislation in Ireland.

www.foi.gov.ie – Freedom of Information Acts are the responsibility for the Department of Public Expenditure and Reform and this is the website for the FOI Central Policy Unit within the Department.

www.ucc.ie/law/lawonline/freedom – This website contains links to a several other sites including FOI legislation, Information Commissioners' web sites, FOI decisions and orders, FOI research centres and NGOs.

www.ocei.gov.ie – Office of the Commissioner for Environmental Information. This is the same as the Information Commissioner under FOI. The website has links to the legislation, speeches by the Commissioner and previous decisions.

www.environ.ie/en/AboutUs/AccesstoInformationontheEnvironment – The Department of the Environment webpage with information on accessing information on the environment.

www.europa.eu/legislation_summaries/environment/general_provi
sions/l28091_en.htm – European Union summary of AIE legislation

http://dataprotection.ie/docs/Home/4.htm – The office of the Data
Protection Commissioner in Ireland. Useful website with lots of
information about seeking personal data and your rights.

www.psi.gov.ie – This is the website for the re-use of public sector
information. It lists all the State organisations that are participating
in PSI and advises how to access it.

UK

www.ico.gov.uk – The office of the Information Commissioner in
the UK. It's an excellent website with advice and details on how to
make FOI applications to bodies in England or Wales. It also the
same body with information on Environmental Information Regulations as AIE is known in the UK.

www.cfoi.org.uk – The home of the Campaign for Freedom of Information in the UK.

www.itspublicknowledge.info/home/Scottishinformationcommissi
oner.asp – Contains information and guidance if you want to find
out about FOI in Scotland – it's the home of the Scottish Information Commissioner. It is also the home for information on EIR.

www.data.gov.uk – This website gives access to a huge amount of
Government information especially details on spending.

www.whatdotheyknow.com – A most interesting website. Allows
you to automatically make and view Freedom of Information requests to all organisations in the UK which are subject to FOI. You

just sign up, fill in the request details and it sends off the request to the relevant authority. Replies come back via the website.

EU/Worldwide

www.asktheeu.org – A really useful website which allows people to submit requests to the EU very easily. Just fill in the request on the website and it sends the request to the correct EU institution. When a reply comes it will bounce it on to the requestor's email and also publishes it on the website.

www.ombudsman.europa.eu – the website for the European Ombudsman. He can investigate claims of maladministration in the bodies and institutions of the European Union. Only citizens of a member state or who live in a member state can make a complaint. For businesses, it is only those with a registered office in the EU that can make a complaint.

www.statewatch.org – An NGO which monitors the EU and its activities from a human rights and open access perspective. The organisation specialists in investigative journalism and critical analysis of the EU particularly in relation to the areas of state, justice, civil liberties and openness.

www.access-info.org – A human rights organisation dedicated to promoting the rights of citizens to access information on the EU and their own governments.

www.privacyinternational.org – An NGO dedicated to raising awareness and protecting people from threats to personal privacy. It also monitors legislation which could infringe on such privacy.
www.foiadvocates.net – The Freedom of Information Advocates Network (FOIAnet) is an international information-sharing net-

work of organizations and individuals working to promote the right of access to information.

www.freedominfo.org – A world wide based organisation of FOI advocates dedicated to promoting openness and FOI in countries. An excellent resource for international FOI.

www.right2info.org – This website brings together information on the legal frameworks for the right to information in more than 100 countries.

www.ifitransparency.org – The Global Transparency Initiative (GTI) is a network of civil society organisations promoting openness in the international financial institutions (IFIs) such as the World Bank, the International Monetary Fund, the European Investment Bank and the Regional Development Banks.

www.foia.gov – A website of the American Department of Justice, it offers a very good introduction to Freedom of Information Acts (FOIA) as it is know in the US.

www.gwu.edu/~nsarchiv – The National Security Archive maintained at the George Washington University. It's an NGO and collects and publishes declassified documents obtained through the Freedom of Information Act. The Archive also serves as a repository of government records on a wide range of topics pertaining to the national security, foreign, intelligence, and economic policies of the United States.

www.aclu.org – Describes itself as the guardian of American liberty at home. The organisation works in the courts and communities to defend and preserve individual rights and liberties, often through the use of FOI.